THE
ACTIVE CATHOLIC

THE
ACTIVE CATHOLIC

(Formerly titled *The Practical Catholic*)

By
Gabriel Palau, S.J.

Translated from the Spanish by
George Charles Hungerford Pollen, S.J.

*"That he might make known unto us the
mystery of his will . . . to re-establish all
things in Christ . . ."*
—Ephesians 1:9-10

TAN BOOKS AND PUBLISHERS, INC.
Rockford, Illinois 61105

Nihil Obstat:

J. N. STRASSMAIER, S.J.

Censor Deputatus

Imprimatur:

EDM. CANONICUS SURMONT,

Vicarius Generalis

Westmonasterii, die 23 Junii, 1910

Published in 1910 by Manresa Press, London, under the title *The Practical Catholic*. Reprinted in 1984 by TAN Books and Publishers, Inc.

Library of Congress Catalog Card No.: 84-50405

ISBN: 0-89555-238-8

Printed and bound in the United States of America.

TAN BOOKS AND PUBLISHERS, INC.
P.O. Box 424
Rockford, Illinois 61105

1984

PONTIFICAL APPROBATION OF THE FIRST EDITION.

Letter from H.E. the Cardinal Secretary of State to the Author:

Rev. Father,

I have the happiness of communicating to you the lively and particular pleasure with which the Holy Father has received the homage of your valuable book entitled *El Católico de Acción*. The Holy Father has observed with satisfaction the deep penetration of this little work, which, although small in size, contains so much of the substance of practical religious life, that it has justly merited the favourable applause of the Spanish Episcopate and it can be fitly indicated as a light and guide to Catholic practice. His Holiness, therefore, through me, thanks you for this filial homage, and, desiring that the good which this little book will do, should redound to its devout author with interest, he sends him with a full heart the Apostolic Benediction.

Thanking you for the copy which you have courteously sent me, I assure you of my sentiments of most sincere esteem, etc.

R. Card. Merry del Val.

Rome, 15th Nov. 1905.

Rev. Father Gabriel Paláu, S.J.
Tortosa.

PREFACE TO THE ENGLISH TRANSLATION.

So many books of devotion have been translated from foreign languages for the use of English-speaking Catholics, that an apology may be called for when another is added to the list. It is, however, hoped that the present work will meet with approval, since it has proved most popular both in the original Spanish and in its French translation.[1] Each of these have run to over 24,000 copies, and each also bears letters of approval and recommendation from the Episcopate.

The author, in his fourth edition, has printed extracts from letters written by three Cardinals, six Archbishops, thirty-one Bishops, and three Administrators of dioceses. Besides these, which are often

[1] The work has also been translated into Italian, Hungarian, Polish (three versions), and Dutch. Versions in Portuguese, German, and Arabic Maronite are in the press.

expressed in the warmest terms, he has a letter from the Cardinal Secretary of State giving him the approbation of His Holiness Pope Pius X., a translation of which is given in the present version.

The aim of this translation has been to reproduce very faithfully the thoughts, and even the words of the author. At the same time, as the whole work is an address of Christ to His disciple, it was desirable to approximate, where possible, to the words and style of the New Testament.

Lastly, it may be well to add that this translation is the only one approved by the author for the British Empire.

CONTENTS.

BOOK I.

Diverte a Malo—"Turn away from Evil."

BOOK II.

Fac Bonum—" Do Good."

BOOK III.

Inquire Pacem—" Seek after Peace."

SPECIAL READINGS FOR PROMOTING CATHOLIC MOVEMENTS.

A. **For works of Christian Economy.**
    Bk. I. ch. 5, 16, 22, 26.
     „   II.   „   1—4, 6, 8, 11, 14, 16.
     „ III.   „   1, 2, 4—6, 8—10, 18.
    See also D.

B. **For Catholic Social Work.**
    Bk. I. ch. 10, 12, 13, 18, 24.
     „   II.   „   1, 8, 10, 14, 16. 21.
     „ III.   „   1—3, 5—8, 10, 13. 14, 21, 22,
                    25, 26.

    See also E.

C. **For Politico-Religious Work.**
    Bk. I. ch. 9, 12, 14, 21, 25.
     „   II.   „   4. 8, 9, 13.
     „ III.   „   11—13, 18, 23.
    See also B and E.

D. **For Moral and Philanthropic Work.**
    Bk. I. ch. 6. 11.
     „   II.   „   3, 7, 11, 12, 14.
     „ III.   „   9, 13.
    See also B and E.

E. **For Propaganda and Defence of the Church.**
    Bk. I. ch. 7, 8, 12, 16, 17, 19, 25.
     „   II.   „   2, 10, 13, 15, 17—19, 21.
     „ III.   „   4, 5. 7, 12, 15, 16, 23, 26.
    See also the preceding.

For Conferences of the Clergy.
    Bk. I. ch. 10, 15—17.
     „   II.   „   6, 9, 13—15, 17, 19.
     „ III.   „   4. 5, 7—11, 13, 15, 17. 18.

READINGS FOR A RETREAT OF EIGHT DAYS.

N.B.—The same chapters may serve for a Retreat of less than eight days, by reading more each day, but in the same order.

THE

ACTIVE CATHOLIC

Instaurare Omnia in Christo—"To
Re-establish All Things in Christ."
—Ephesians 1:10

BOOK THE FIRST.

Diverte a malo—"Turn away from evil."

Psalm xxxiii. 15.

CHAPTER I.

OF WISDOM MORE USEFUL THAN ALL KNOWLEDGE WHICH I CAN ACQUIRE.

1. My words are sweet as honey to those who love My teaching, and keep My commandments.

2. But My voice is a raging tempest which uprooteth the cedars of Lebanon, to those who despise My counsels and think themselves great, when they sin in their knowledge.

3. Iniquity doth but triumph to its ruin: justice ever to its glory.

4. The wicked man lifteth himself to have a greater fall, and the just man abaseth himself to be raised on high.

5. The proud will hear My word, but will not understand its meaning.

6. The humble will listen to My teaching, and will rest consoled therein.

7. The more My words sink into thee, the more wilt thou ponder them in thy heart.

8. The more the ungodly philosopher be puffed up with pride, the less he perceiveth what My works reveal.

9. He alone will hear My voice with profit, and he alone will understand what I am saying to him, who, thinking little of his own knowledge, hungereth after Eternal Truth and the science of the Saints.

10. Then will human science profit him much, since all truth beareth witness to My goodness and My wisdom.

11. Then will the humble man be learned, and the learned man of pure heart be humble.

12. Humility giveth more light to man's mind than all vain learning that feedeth men's pride.

13. To learn for learning's sake is vanity, if good works are wanting in thy life.

14. To learn for the sake of vain appearance is vanity of vanities, and vexation of mind.

15. To learn for the sake of injuring the simple is the deceit and malice of the proud.

16. Blessed are those who believe, for they will understand many mysteries of life and will not fall into the snares of false philosophers.

17. Blessed are the learned men who are humble, for they shall possess the wisdom of the Faith which enlighteneth the heart, and

as shining beacons they shall be useful to their fellow-men in the problems of life.

18. The believer who can humbly teach his brother, will find consolation in My teaching and the spirit of life in the midst of My words.

19. If the Lord of knowledge deign to enlighten thee, make thyself an apostle in truth according to thy state.

20. And the more thou learn of the Church, the more humble wilt thou be in thy judgments and the more secure in thy learning.

CHAPTER II.

HOW THE LORD INTENDETH MY COMFORT AND REPOSE.

1. If thou desire to taste the manna of the spirit, withdraw thyself apart, where thou mayest converse freely with Me.

2. Many have not yet tasted spiritual delights, and therefore easily yield to the allurements of the flesh.

3. One hour of heavenly consolation is worth more than all the feasts of this world.

4. Then wilt thou know the inner joy of the spirit, when thou withdrawest from the tumult of the crowd.

5. He who would work with Me and for My Cause, must sometimes withdraw into retirement.

6. Deem not that thou hast done great things for God, until thou hast learned how sweet it is to be alone in My presence.

7. Some believe they do much amongst men, because they make much stir, yet have they not that heat which enkindleth souls.

8. Say not: "I cannot be recollected, I have no time:" if it be true that thy many occupations oppress thee, this is the very reason why thou shouldst withdraw for some days.

9. I always ordained that My Apostles should rest, so that their spirit might not grow feeble.

10. Thou wilt do more for Me and for thyself by one hour of earnest meditation, than by whole days of empty discussion and study.

11. I am He who enlighteneth the depths of the soul: I am He who strengtheneth the recesses of the mind.

12. Of more profit is one truth well under-

stood, than a thousand ingenious discourses and brilliant fancies.

13. Dost thou not perceive at every step, how many new and learned things are uttered by the lips of proud philosophers? Yet with all that, their pride is so great, that they know not what this meaneth—to live for the true life.

CHAPTER III.

IN HOW MANY WAYS MY MASTER INVITETH AND DRAWETH ME TO HIM.

1. Son, if thou conform slavishly to the present world, thou becomest the slave of this world.

2. Learn to guide thyself, learn to be superior to fleeting things, and thou wilt walk upon the waters.

3. He who knoweth not how to rule himself, is like a ship without a rudder, exposed to the fury of the winds.

4. He who cannot turn from seductive charms, taketh his own way to his death.

5. He who feareth overmuch, sinketh himself by his own weight into the abyss.

6. Man of little faith, why dost thou place thyself in danger to no purpose?

7. Have confidence if thou dost practise: practise if thou believest: believe if thou hast judgment and reason.

8. Do not trouble thyself without cause, nor let fears disturb thee.

9. If thy judgment blind thee, of what use to thee are thy senses?

10. And if thy senses mislead thee, what profit dost thou draw from the light of Mine eyes?

11. I watch thee everywhere, and yet thy heart doth not seek Me.

12. If the serpent hath bitten thee, wherefore still caress him?

13. If his venom hath poisoned thee, wherefore shun the antidote?

14. If men have led thee astray, wherefore persist in following them?

15. Learn to read, and to cease to read.

16. Learn to open thine ears, and to stop them.

17. Learn to contemplate Me, and to curb thine own desires.

18. Hast thou denied Me? Why then dost thou not weep?

19. Hast thou caused Me to be blasphemed? Why then dost thou not confess Me?

20. If thou hast loved vanity, why lovest thou not the true Love?

21. Purify thy heart, and thou shalt rest on My bosom.

22. In it I will tell thee of the Kingdom of Love, and of the workings of the heart.

23. And with it thou shalt labour and conquer and transform, and thou shalt do prodigies for the good of men.

24. If thou desire to be My friend, give thyself to Me without reserve, and My grace shall work in thee, that thou mayest work with Me.

CHAPTER IV.

THAT I MUST BE VERY CONSISTENT IN FOLLOWING MY MASTER.

1. Son, thou speakest much and dost little.

2. Thou givest Me some things, and keepest thyself for thyself.

3. Thou desirest that I may be known and honoured, so thou sayest, and thou thinkest ever of thine own glory.

4. Thou bewailest the sins of the world, and thou dost not weep for thine own.

5. Thou canst find fault with all, but thou dost not amend thyself.

6. Thou sayest to Me, "My God, I love Thee," and, thereafter, thou dost not serve Me.

7. Thou deplorest the persistent fury of My determined enemies, and thou applaudest and extollest their talents and enlightenment.

8. Thou desirest Me "above all things," and presently thou deniest this in practice.

9. Many times thou deniest Me rather than deny thyself.

10. And at other times thou deniest thyself rather than deny My greatest enemies.

11. Thou desirest interior happiness and consolation, and thou seekest worldly amusements.

12. All things thou hast are Mine, and thou turnest them into playthings.

13. Thou puttest the earthly and trifling before the eternal and divine, and thou desirest to be very Catholic.

14. To-day thou wouldst labour well to ensure thy salvation, and to-morrow thou labourest ill, and hardly wilt thou own that thou mayest be lost.

15. At one time thou desirest to go to

Heaven, and at another thou desirest that there were no Hell.

16. Of what use to thee are thy devotions, if thou do not raise thyself above thy desires and passions?

17. What profit dost thou draw from good emotions, if thy works are not good?

18. How canst thou be a Christian, if human respect prevail so much against thee?

19. Thou desirest to be a Catholic in private for thine own sake, and I ask thee to be a Catholic in public and for My sake.

20. Ah, My son, how often dost thou desire to be virtuous, and how often, alas, dost thou contradict thyself!

CHAPTER V.

OF LIGHT THAT I CAN OBTAIN FROM CERTAIN TRUTHS AND ERRORS.

1. When principle is wanting, there is excess of show; and when there is excess of show, vanity possesseth the whole.

2. When submission is wanting, men make a great parade; and when men make

a great parade, misery maketh its home in their dwellings.

3. When truth is wanting, truths are much disputed; and when truths are much disputed, hearts and fields grow barren.

4. When religion is wanting, matter rebelleth and ruleth; and when matter rebelleth and ruleth, men live like the beasts.

5. When the spirit is wanting, there is much flesh; and when there is much flesh, weakness possesseth the body.

6. What doth it profit to develop taste, if thou become the slave of concupiscence?

7. What doth liberty profit, if thou lose freedom of spirit?

8. What do honours profit, if thy passions be flattered?

9. What do great things profit, if thou stumble over little things?

10. What doth it profit to have many things, if thou lose the good thing?

11. What doth it profit to have the better, if thou live the worse?

12. What doth it profit to live, if thou waste thy time?

13. Folly of follies is it to have understanding and not to know how to live as a Christian.

14. Thou must examine thyself; thou must reprove thyself; thou must subject thyself; thou must refrain thyself.

15. By patience, by purity, by humility, by charity, by the virtue most wanting in thee, which is the one that is most repugnant to thee, and most displeaseth thee in thine opponents—by these thou must force thy way, with a firm and rapid step, to Heaven.

CHAPTER VI.

OF THE MOST PROFITABLE WAY OF DEALING WITH OUR OWN AFFAIRS.

1. The angels fell because they would not acknowledge Me; men shall fall that do not acknowledge Me. But if thy brother fall through thy fault, I will ask an account of his soul from thee.

2. And if thine injustice ruin many, thou shalt pay for all.

3. Anger above anger is My wrath on him who injureth My people.

4. I am the Majesty the most terrible against the unjust and the mighty.

5. I am the God ever incensed and

hidden from him who causeth My name to be blasphemed.

6. My words are the voice of justice for the poor and for the rich.

7. If thy brother have sinned by thine excess, save many by thine example and virtues.

8. And if many have sinned through thy teaching, save thine own soul by condemning thine errors seventy-fold.

9. Moreover, if thou hast abused thy power over many to mislead or injure the simple, make thyself the slave of all, of the poor and of the rich.

10. Wherefore dost thou desire liberty, if thou use it not to destroy iniquity?

11. The slave of self can only free himself by submitting to My law.

12. I am the Father of the poor, and He who exalteth the humble.

13. I am the voice of the simple, and the peace of the peace-makers.

14. If the poor man sin against himself, for his greater misfortune, I may for once allow him to grow rich.

15. But if he sin against the rich, he shall not escape from his misery, until he be doubly poor and wretched.

16. Yet woe to the rich man who sinneth

against the poor, his riches shall be a weight of iniquity, and his heavy injustices as ropes of steel, dragging him to the abyss.

17. No man will mock at God in the day of the revelation of His justice.

18. I will render to each one according to his works, and to what side each one leaneth, to that shall he fall.

19. Redeem then thy slavery before the time; give alms for thy sins.

20. Give of what thou hast, and what thou hast not shall be given to thee.

21. Blessed is he that shall do good to souls; more blessed is he that shall do good to souls and bodies.

22. Wise in truth is he that knoweth how to do good.

23. Very prudent for himself is he who striveth to do good to his brother.

24. And very prudent for all men is he who honoureth and supporteth My ministers, because all profit by these honours and all have honour from that support.

25. He who hath received more, must give more, and he who hath the more offended My justice, must the more honour My goodness.

CHAPTER VII.

1. What doth it matter to thee if others neglect their charge, if they prosper or fail, or if they continue silent?

2. Have I made thee a shepherd of the flock? Art thou doing all that thou oughtest to oppose the attacks of the wolf?

3. It is useless to trouble about those matters whereof thou wilt have no account to give in the day of reward and punishment.

4. He who is much occupied, freeth himself from many rash judgments.

5. Take heed to thyself and to doctrine, and thou wilt see that thou art dust, and that thou hast nought wherein to glorify thyself, or to contemn thy superiors and thine equals.

6. He who is much occupied and is intent on that which occupieth him, will observe few, if any, of the faults of others.

7. Many fancy that to be zeal which only ariseth from a vain desire of pleasing themselves.

8. Many believe that they have My spirit,

but they only act on the impulse of their own nature.

9. Many think overmuch of defending their own ideas, but few of humbling and amending themselves.

10. I am He who knoweth all things, and I shall give to each one his deserts.

11. Not all that seemeth virtue is virtue : when a man speaketh much of himself and his own affairs, some fault easily lieth hidden within his work.

12. Do thou follow Me, and attend to thy work : why dost thou afflict thyself with useless cares ?

13. When a man hath greatness of soul and uprightness of intention, he doth not easily over-rate himself, nor doth he desist from good works for small or mean objects.

14. It will serve thee but little towards becoming more humble and diligent, if thou notice and consider that others do not work as they should, nor esteem highly that which thou esteemest.

15. If others wash not their hands, and this seemeth to thee a falling off from holiness and right conduct, see that thou neglect not to have thy heart very clean.

16. Many times scandals arise, and the

simple become disobedient through the fault of those that murmur.

17. Before speaking, weigh very carefully if it would not be better and more profitable to keep silence.

18. If thou desire greatly that thou shouldst do much, and that others should do more than thou, then would it please thee that the works of others should obtain more glory than thine own.

19. When a man is very humble in mind and spirit, he will not thrust himself forward to judge others, unless he have authority so to do, nor will he be keen to examine if they have fulfilled their duty.

20. Watch thy steps and thou wilt see how far thou still art from true charity, and from following the path that the Apostles trod.

21. If thou art much drawn to judging, and it seemeth to thee that thy judgment be good, fulfil what hath been commanded thee so often, under My grace and Mine inspiration, and thou shalt have part with the judges in the day when the humble shall be glorified.

CHAPTER VIII.

SOME WORDS OF THE LORD, WHICH MOVE
ME DEEPLY.

1. Oh error and vanity above all errors and all vanities, to imagine ye labour for My glory, whilst remaining in sin.

2. When the moment cometh of the revelation of My glory, how can I draw glory to Myself from the works of My servant, if he himself hath not kept My commandments?

3. Many there are who seem to be doing, when in truth they are but contradicting themselves and undoing.

4. One single sin from one of those who call Me Lord and Master, grieveth Me more than a thousand from My greatest enemies.

5. Be ye holy as I am holy, and ye shall be truly apostles, and your works shall be fruitful, and your zealous apostolate shall be regarded as divine.

6. If he who owneth himself a sinner, offend Me, it is truly a great injury to himself: but if he who professeth to be My follower, sin and repent not, it is a great injury to Me as well.

7. Think not that thou hast done any

profitable work for My Church, if thou have not full right, from thine own state of soul, to proclaim the glory that My grace meriteth.

8. It mattereth little that a man hath been a sinner in the past, if he have done due penance : but it mattereth much that he live without sin now for the good name of My Cause.

9. Watch well then what thou thinkest : watch what thou sayest : abhor all that is disordinate in thy desires and evil in thy deeds.

10. I know what I expect from thee, and would to Heaven thou didst attain it, for My aims are very high, and thou knowest Me not yet.

11. If thou feel troubled, I am the only One that can truly console thee ; if thou feel at peace and happy, I am the only one that can ensure the fulness of thy joy.

12. Hear and weigh My words : thou shalt find Me everywhere.

13. If thou work well, thou shalt find joy in My words : if thou work ill, in these also shalt thou find a remedy.

14. My voice is a two-edged sword that woundeth and healeth at the same time for the good of My friends.

15. Let not vain fears trouble thee. If thou understand not what passeth in thy spirit, be very humble, open thy conscience, and thou shalt find in humility that which science cannot obtain.

16. Many times the sufferings of the mind proceed from the body; at other times, the sufferings of the body proceed from the mind.

17. It is not given to all to understand these things, but I teach the humble that which oft-times the proud and presumptuous do not succeed in understanding.

18. Greatly do I esteem true science, and for this reason, I place it in humility, so that it may be more sure, more stable, and more free from all admixture of error and all vanity of dogmatizing.

19. Be very humble, and thou shalt be pure, and thou shalt be upright, and thou shalt be wise, and thy deeds shall be true and shall bear fruit.

CHAPTER IX.

OF A VERY SURE WAY OF CORRECTING MYSELF AND OF BECOMING USEFUL.

1. Thou hast yet much to learn, My son, if thou seek to labour rightly.

2. Thou wilt know how to rejoice, when thou hast learned how to weep.

3. Thou wilt know how to weep with profit, when thou knowest the evil thou hast done.

4. Thou wilt know the evil thou hast done and which thou oughtest to avoid, when thou knowest the good that thou hadst to do.

5. Thou wilt know the good that thou hadst to do, when thou knowest who I am that placed thee in this world, and why I have given thee being.

6. Oh, didst thou often reflect on these things, how much wouldst thou advance in the school of prudence!

7. Answer Me: what will it profit thee to have been a Christian in name, or to have had only the outward semblance of a just man?

8. Many speak of honour and honesty,

and do not reflect that such words will be their most terrible accusers at the Judgment.

9. Oh, what vanity and malice are hidden under a very beautiful and virtuous appearance!

10. Think much on thy faults, and thou wilt not fear sacrifices.

11. Think much on My Passion, and thou wilt no longer yield to thy passions.

12. Think much and labour much, and thy understanding will not be a barren field.

13. At times thou wouldst desire to do something for My glory, but thou fearest to fall into some sin.

14. If thy weakness be so great, still more hurtful to thy soul would idleness be.

15. Be humble and prudent, and thou wilt conquer.

16. If thou canst do nought in person and in deed, work by thine influence and by thine alms.

17. If thou canst not write, thou canst speak; and if thou canst not speak, thou canst pray.

18. If thou canst not teach by set discourses, thou canst always give a good example.

19. As Death ever maketh a way for himself, so shouldst thou ever advance towards the death of thy vices.

20. No lot in this world is happier than that of those Christians who strive to ensure their salvation more and more by an abundance of good works.

21. Doth the fear of Hell at times overcome thee? Put thyself in a state of grace, live in grace, co-operate with grace, make thyself the apostle of My grace, and thou shalt suffer no injury from this eternal evil and greatest of all misfortunes.

22. But thou art oppressed by the thought, whether thou art yet pardoned! Work for My glory, and thou wilt be freed from thy doubts; I never deny salvation to those who sincerely seek My ways, nor do I deny peace to those who devote themselves to labour.

CHAPTER X.

THAT I CAN PROFIT MUCH FROM MY PAST FAULTS.

1. If thou think to do much in punctiliously defending the honours and rights of thine office, thy folly and vanity will find no excuse in Mine eyes.

2. The wicked prowl around thy flock to

ruin them by flattery; and thou thinkest to do much by showing a very bad humour and much vexation of mind.

3. Wouldst thou see what beseemeth thy true dignity? Set aside thy great ambitions, and Love will give thee a hundredfold.

4. Thou must not set forth with hurtful aims, nor with base flattery to gain the hearts of men.

5. What pleaseth most and speaketh best are humble virtues and virtuous deeds.

6. How canst thou be despised, if thou knowest how to love?

7. Thou must not, however, look upon kind and considerate manners as vain and useless.

8. Man is very weak, and the poorer and feebler he is, the more eagerly he desireth to be loved.

9. Do not fall into the vice of vulgar souls, by showing thyself over-rigid to others and over-accommodating to thyself in the discharge of thine office.

10. Tell Me how those under thee live, and I will tell thee what faults thou hast.

11. Tell Me how thou thyself livest, and what dislikes thou hast, and I will tell thee the virtues thou hast not.

12. If thou once despise thine equals, thou wilt often receive insults.

13. If thou cease to obey thy lawful superiors, the lowest of the people will refuse thee obedience.

14. If thou cease to fulfil small duties, thou wilt one day have great regrets.

15. Son, if thou often salute others, thou wilt merit that they one day repay thee thy salutations.

16. Son, if thou respect the lowly, respect will one day be shown thee by the great.

17. Son, how canst thou teach, if thou hast not learnt to correct thyself? And how canst thou correct others, if thou hast not amended thyself?

18. If thou seek love, then sow love: and if thou desire thy rights, then make thy duties fruitful.

19. My son, if thou despise My lessons, then must I teach thee with rods.

20. Remember that when thou wast not seeking Me, I was seeking thee.

21. Remember that when thou wast not regarding Me, I was regarding thee.

22. Remember that when thou wast not inviting Me, I was entering the door of thy house.

23. Remember that when thou didst ask for a benefit, I gave thee My grace.

24. Thou didst only desire favour, and I gave thee My Self!

25. If thou wouldst be grateful to Me, do much good to My bitterest enemies.

26. Son, a thousand times My son, there are many sinners in the world: for what low and wretched things dost thou delay to make thyself a great saint?

CHAPTER XI.

OF SOME THINGS WHICH I MUST FORSAKE SO AS NOT TO BE LOST.

1. If I have bidden thee to follow Me, wherefore dost thou wish to delay?

2. That which hindereth thee to-day, will be thy ruin to-morrow.

3. That which to-day thou embracest with inordinate love, will be thy torment to-morrow.

4. There is one good above every good; seek it truly, and thou shalt obtain all good.

5. It is little that the world can give thee: its greatest treasures are the empty promises it maketh to thee.

6. See that thou use all things according to My will, and no passing matters of this world shall injure thee.

7. The best use thou canst make of all earthly things is to lay them at the feet of the Apostles.

8. If thou knowest how to trample underfoot the vanities of this life, then of a truth thou hast sound judgment.

9. If creatures do not help thee to find Me, whereto do they profit thee?—To follow after those who have left the right way.

10. Thou seest this man, who seemeth so mighty and yet is so depraved? Know that a child, who dieth in baptismal grace, is greater than he.

11. Many would be better than they are, if they were less rich.

12. No greater misfortune can befall a man, than to lose virtues and the gifts of grace for the treasures of this world.

13. Wealth, power, majesty, learning, genius, are great misfortunes to him who turneth to evil what might have served for the good of so many.

14. Oh, vanity of vanities, to pretend to please Me by merely external show!

15. Oh, vanity of vanities, to imagine that thou art esteemed by that world which only despiseth thee for thy vices!

16. Oh, vanity of vanities, to use thy strength in order to crush the weak!

17. A day will come when virtues will rise up against thee, and from afar shalt thou watch the poor seat themselves at My table.

18. If thou takest delight in disorder, do not forget that many are suffering where there never can be order.

CHAPTER XII.

OF CERTAIN GREAT ERRORS THAT AT TIMES I LABOUR UNDER.

1. He who will listen to My counsels, will not easily fall into great errors.

2. It is a great error to hurl insults; since they neither injure the wicked, nor edify the simple, nor bring honour on him that hurleth them.

3. It is a great error to exact as certain and necessary that which the Church leaveth free, and considereth probable and of less importance.

4. It is a great error to desire to go with haste, or towards a side, where the Church goeth slowly and taketh a middle course.

5. It is a great error to boast of fidelity and zeal to My Vicar; and, when in conflict

and doubt, to refuse direct appeals and prayers to him.

6. It is a great error for a man to claim to interpret the instructions of My Church, in order to defend his personal interests, or from inordinate love of controversy.

7. It is a great error to seek to vindicate righteousness and truth when a man lacketh prudence, humility, and charity.

8. It is a great error to set thyself to judge and define obscure issues, when passion disturbeth thy reason, or when hatred causeth thee to see as certainties what are only suspicions and doubts.

9. It is a great error to cast accusations on others, when a man is silent on his own sins, and excuseth what he ought to be the first to deplore and confess.

10. It is a great error to cry out at sin and scandal when it is even yet unknown how far the malice extendeth.

11. It is a great error to apply violent remedies when the sickness can be cured by more gentle medicine.

12. It is a great error to tolerate errors when they occasion scandal and can cause or foment worse ills.

13. It is a great error for a man to show himself exceedingly severe towards his breth-

ren, and in his own affairs to be ever indulgent.

14. It is a great error to think of glorious victories when the weapons are neither dignified nor honest.

15. It is a great error to insist on crying out when My Vicar commandeth silence.

16. It is a great error to think of triumph in the end, if a man do not labour for a partial victory now.

17. It is a great error to say: "We must have all or nothing," when impiety invadeth all step by step.

18. It is a great error vainly to trust that good hath power to spring from the abyss of ill.

19. I alone draw good out of evil, but never will I do this to condone ill-concealed sloth, nor do I reward those who earn no prize.

20. The humble and peace-loving man doth more for My glory than the quarrelsome and proud.

21. He who laboureth, doth more for My honour than he who resteth on his laurels.

22. He who watcheth, doth more for My name than he who slumbereth much and hopeth much.

23. He who suffereth a wrong for My

Cause, doth more than he who wrestleth with all the strength of a giant.

24. Error of errors is it to defend sanctity, whilst living in sin and secretly rejoicing in evil.

25. If in truth thou art zealous and practical, bethink thee twice of what thou must say, be silent on what thou must conceal, begin thine undertakings at the beginning, and ever demand more, little by little, with firmness and sweetness.

CHAPTER XIII.

THAT I MUST RISE TO THE HEIGHTS OF DIVINE THOUGHT.

1. Cease, My son, to bewail the powerful influence of vice and the strength of the weapons wherewith the wicked contend.

2. Every evil seemeth to thee very great and most terribly powerful.

3. Every disorder appeareth to thee more stable and more secure than good order;

4. Every lie more able than the truth to captivate the reason, every vice more alluring than virtue to gain the heart.

5. Oh, man, of a faith more human than divine! Oh, Christian of wavering trust!

6. What transformed the pagan world, but the faith of humble Christians?

7. What caused self-sacrifice to be loved, but the poverty of the follower of Christ?

8. What made the little great, the weak strong, the simple wise, but the charity of the Apostles, who a little before had hid themselves?

9. He who denied Me, confessed Me: He who persecuted Me more than all, proclaimed Me.

10. All My Apostles gave their lives, and the world was converted.

11. I taught a doctrine opposed to the maxims of the world, and the slaves were set free.

12. I taught a truth till then unheard, and the great masters of paganism learned it from My lowly disciples.

13. I taught a morality which restrained, a virtue which hid itself, a knowledge which humbled itself, a charity the happier the more it gave away, and the school of the Cross transformed the world into a school of sacrifice and heroism.

14. I reached the summit of Calvary, and

I placed the most despised of earth above the heights of Heaven.

15. Children became giants and overcame the power of their tormentors.

16. The great ones became humble and served their slaves.

17. The cruel became humane and tended the sick.

18. Masters made themselves slaves for the good of captives, and in their fetters found themselves more free, more masters of themselves than ever.

19. The flesh produced flowers of angelic virtues, and the spirit triumphed over Hell.

20. And thou art still carnal! And thine eyes are blinded!

21. If thou see not the marvels of grace, make thyself a spiritual man.

22. One virtue can do more than a thousand vices, and it is the more powerful in practice the more it is allied to sacrifice.

23. One truth achieveth more than a thousand lies, and it attaineth the greater splendour of victory, the more it is enforced by practical example.

24. The power of prayer obtaineth more than a thousand efforts of the learned, and the more it oppose evil, the more will it trust in humility.

25. Thou shalt find help in natural means, when thou believest in the power of the supernatural.

26. Thou wilt see little, and thou wilt be easily terrified, if thou do not rise to the heights of Divine Thought. Pray much, and in humble trust shalt thou find the way.

CHAPTER XIV.

HOW I MUST ENLIGHTEN MYSELF SO AS NOT TO FALL INTO ERROR.

1. Son, if someone be opposed to thee, or thou feel aversion towards him, watch well how thou bearest thyself with him, for he may easily seem more hostile to thee and worse than he is in reality.

2. A careful examination of our own faults is a great remedy against seeing, or for excusing those of others.

3. Thou wilt easily believe that others have false principles, if they do not in all things conform to thine own.

4. Thou canst without danger judge and condemn another when he consciously and clearly judgeth and condemneth himself.

5. Nevertheless, it is good that thou be on the watch. For easily and without pain doth the serpent bite.

6. That Arch-Enemy of man is perpetually on the watch to entrap the unwary, the self-sufficient, and the ambitious, by false reasoning and apparent good.

7. Distrust all teachings which lead thee astray, and all promises which do not amend thee.

8. Fear not that which helpeth to restrain thee, nor the truths which rebuke thee.

9. There is much vanity in all changing systems, but the truth is ever simple and steadfast.

10. Much shouldst thou distrust him who flattereth thee, above all if it trouble or disturb thee.

11. Much shouldst thou fear conceits and ambitions which do not render thee more exact in thy duties.

12. True liberty existeth only in My Church; for the truths of faith establish and protect it.

13. Woe to those that misuse the truths of science, for they will end in darkness.

14. To enjoy much is not progress, but rather to suffer more patiently.

15. He is wise in truth, who humbleth

himself often, and walketh along the true path.

16. He loveth men in truth, who sacrificeth himself for their eternal salvation.

17. He loveth the liberty of all, who perfectly fulfilleth My laws.

18. If thou practise virtue, thou wilt learn much, more than all the learned who teach only vanity and folly.

19. If thou knowest many things concerning this world, thou still knowest nothing profitable, if thou know not how to examine thy conscience.

20. And if thou thinkest thou hast done marvels, thou hast done little, if thou hast not done due penance for thy sins.

21. Happy is the unlearned man who setteth his life in order, but more happy the wise man who reformeth himself.

22. He who knoweth little, if he be not very holy, can do little; he who knoweth much, if he be not very holy, of what use to him is his knowledge?

23. Alas, what a terrible account will some have to give in the great day when the consciences of all shall be laid bare!

CHAPTER XV.

HOW I MUST AVOID EXTREMES TO GO THE STRAIGHT WAY.

1. My son, when thou feelest the fervour of zeal, beware of the excesses of the evil Spirit.

2. Thou wilt know that thou art inspired by the good Spirit, if thou be master of thyself.

3. Many do nothing profitable, through failing to follow the straight road.

4. They think to labour for My Cause, and the spirit of confusion possesseth them.

5. They think that all is an apostolate, yet they never effect the conversion of one soul.

6. They think that outcries can do much, and the more they cry out and agitate, the less doth the crowd heed what they say.

7. They take their inspiration from turbulent men, and follow but little the example of My saints.

8. If it be needful to destroy, much more is it right to build up.

9. If it be needful to attack, much more is it right to instruct.

10. If thou art intent only on making evil known, when wilt thou teach wherein consisteth true good?

11. Thou art right in opposing the evil deeds of the wicked, yet the splendour of virtue and good works availeth more than the thunder of denunciation and invective.

12. None can believe that it is the spirit of the Gospel to wound and wound again, and not to apply any remedy to the wounds.

13. The truly spiritual man can do more than a powerful general.

14. More victories are gained by winning hearts than by attacking with cannons.

15. Drastic remedies, too long pursued, bring death, rather than combat the malady.

16. Oh, if thou hadst the true spirit of zeal! How many souls wouldst thou win for My Cause and for Heaven!

17. Then wouldst thou be neither feeble nor impetuous;

18. Then wouldst thou be neither cowardly nor presumptuous;

19. Then wouldst thou know how to deal with every soul;

20. Then wouldst thou labour, not at the bidding of passion, but at the dictates of reason.

21. Where there is neither method nor

organisation, even in doing good there is loss of time.

22. Hold ever the greatest and most sublime ideals, and apply the most practical means.

23. And if thou desire to know what is most practical and profitable, ask Me for that which is most profitable for thy neighbour, and most full of sacrifice and labour for thyself.

CHAPTER XVI.

HOW TO ENCOURAGE MYSELF, IF MY STRENGTH GROWETH WEAK.

1. Why is thy heart troubled? Already it seemeth to thee that all is lost.

2. Already thou desirest to rest from thy labours, or to have come into the world in another age.

3. Thus have always argued men little instructed and weak-minded.

4. See and contemplate the work of My Church throughout the ages; that which appeared at one time to be defeat was but the work of preparing another victory.

5. Those are true triumphs, which are held for such by future ages.

6. Those are glorious victories, which are won with inferior weapons.

7. Those are profitable results, in which good overcometh great evils.

8. What remaineth of the mighty and exalted ones of the past? Their memory only liveth to bear witness to the existence and persistence of My Church.

9. Mine is an all-powerful providence; there is no power which can resist it.

10. If I allow successive calamities, if I permit terrible storms, if I suffer the winds to rush together and the waves of the sea to rage, it is that the triumph of My Church may be gained only by the power of My words, and that the faith of the humble may be strengthened.

11. Much shalt thou learn from bygone times, and history will teach thee by its many pages.

12. If evils seem to thee to be greater to-day, watch well that thy perverse enemies do not exaggerate them.

13. But even if they are greater than in the past, the more glorious will be the victory, and the more fruitful its effects.

14. If thou art attentive to evil, forget not to contemplate the greatness of good.

15. Partial defeats are the shades which make the final victory stand out.

16. If all were well, if there were no enemies, there would be few virtues and great vices in the world.

17. Then are there saints, and greater saints, when there are greater combats.

18. All things serve in the end so that the progress of My Church should be more glorious.

19. If thy mind raise itself to the heights of faith and knowledge, if thou think not of self, I promise thee, thou shalt contemplate wondrous marvels.

20. Then, far from being paralyzed with fear, thou wilt praise Me and believe; and thy soul, as the dove, shall fly above the flood of evil.

CHAPTER XVII.

HOW I MUST STUDY THE INTERIOR LIFE IN ORDER TO SUCCEED WITH THE EXTERIOR.

1. My son, thou hast not yet taken to heart that three brave souls are worth more than three hundred cowards.

2. Thou hast not yet grasped the truth that one fervent Christian can achieve far

more than hundreds who are remiss or luke-warm.

3. Thou hast not yet tested what a union of brothers can do, whom the love of charity uniteth.

4. Little dost thou know of that fervour which springeth, not from fulness of outward life, but from the charity which dwelleth within the spirit.

5. If thou succeed in placing thyself above the changes and failures of external things, it is a great sign of virtue and of what great works thou canst perform.

6. If a man to-day be full of zeal and feel that he could cast the heavy mass of a mountain into the deep, let him be on his guard that to-morrow he be not so cowardly that he dare not go out into the street.

7. Men of little faith are so weak that to-day they forget to beg the favour of My grace, and to-morrow they will importune Me with cries for help, and will desert their work.

8. The man who is prudent and enlightened doth not give himself up to excess of fervour, nor doth he disturb himself for the hurrahs or hisses of the wicked.

9. When thou desirest to undertake any

work, observe carefully the difficulty of the obstacles and the excellence of the project.

10. If through pleasure or displeasure thou begin to neglect the good which I inspire, thou shalt do nothing.

11. Pleasure cometh and goeth, and displeasure is ever at hand.

12. I satisfy what is above pleasure; foster the desire to please Me, and to be of use to the brethren.

13. If thou canst be free from pleasing thyself and seeking thyself in thine undertakings, do not doubt but that thou hast found the key to consolations.

14. One drop of honey produced by the bees of heaven is worth more than all earthly banquets and delights.

15. Thou savourest little the things of thy God, if thou yet relish or desire the delights of the world.

16. Thou must not, however, abandon thyself without measure to consolations of spirit, nor afflict thyself overmuch when thou findest them not in the service of God, for to make too much of them impedeth rather than profiteth.

17. Neither oughtest thou to afflict thyself overmuch because thou producest little fruit, nor shouldst thou rejoice without measure when thine undertakings succeed.

18. If thine affairs go badly, or do not yield the abundance of good that thou didst hope, seek out diligently whence this impediment cometh and redouble the fervour of thy spirit.

19. If all go according to thy desires, it is well to discover what may be useful at other times, and above all, cease not to humble thyself and to labour with constancy.

CHAPTER XVIII.

THAT IN OUTWARDLY PROMOTING UNION WITH MY BRETHREN, I SHALL FIND MANY BENEFITS.

1. He who saith that he defendeth the strict purity of My doctrine, let him watch well that he expose not to scorn the sincerity of My Cause.

2. He who applieth bad means in favour of My Church, let him know for certain that he maketh himself My greatest enemy.

3. He who relinquisheth the weapons of the just and honest man, let him ask himself whether he be very holy or very foolish.

4. He who stumbleth at every step, and

only findeth faults in others, let him see well if he walk uprightly, and if he examine his conscience.

5. It is better to do little, and to continue with constancy, than to undertake many things and to abandon them.

6. It is better to begin with a prospect of success something not so perfect, than to aim at the more perfect and effect nothing.

7. He who receiveth Communion with others in humble fervour, serveth Me better than he who standeth aloof and spendeth his strength in loud sighs.

8. The Sacraments are outward signs of the graces they confer : they are the best means for social union in My Church.

9. Oh, if My disciples who live in the world were always true Christians !

10. Nothing is more social than the Religion that I have founded ; nothing so united and so full of life as the Body of which I am the Head.

11. I united My Apostles : I united My disciples : I united men : I united women. And I have joined the rich with the poor, and the wise with the unlearned, and the great with the small, and the slaves with the free, and the Gentiles with the converted Jews.

12. I am the Way of true progress : I am the Truth which enlighteneth every sane reason : I am the Life who giveth true life, very human, very social, and supernatural.

13. I am come to bestow life abundantly, to raise from the dead souls and bodies alike.

14. I am the Civilization of peoples, and He Who brought Heaven near to the solitary.

15. If there be order, it is from Me ; and if there be disorder, it is from man and the Enemy of the human race.

16. If there be truth in science ; if there be an answer to problems ; if a solution to calculations ; and if there be love among men, and if peace resteth upon the nation, and virtues flourish, all is from Me, and the truth of these glories will give eloquent testimony of My truth and My glory.

17. All good which separateth itself from the Highest Good, or which raiseth itself independently to make itself the highest good, will be an apparent good and a true evil : and only by being destroyed and ruined will it give glory to My Justice : and it will deplore the ingratitude of its works when it learneth the furthest limits of My Mercy.

18. Oh, what sorry Catholics are those who are of no service for the cloister, nor for

solitary life, nor for the social life of this world, the life of exterior union in charity!

19. The offering of My true Sacrifice is a social work: and Christians think not of assisting with My minister to offer in social union to My Father the Host which the priest offereth in their name.

20. The "Our Father" is a social work, and My sons do not recite it in common with united hearts.

21. The Holy Communion of My true Body is a social work, and Christians do not communicate in one body as having one spirit.

22. The Communion of Saints is a social work for the good of those that combat in My Church, and Christians have no common trust in the union of brotherhood and in the prayers of their brothers.

23. I have joined man to God, and earth to Heaven, and the children of Adam to My grace; and I abhor the malice and the disorder of sin, because it destroyeth every lasting bond of union and all true brotherly and social happiness of man.

24. I have chosen you for disciples, I have called you friends and brothers, I have esteemed you as sons; and where is the glory of your names, and where the works worthy of such high titles?

CHAPTER XIX.

THAT I MUST BEGIN BY ESTABLISHING
MYSELF IN GOOD IF I WOULD EFFECT
MUCH GOOD.

1. Many things have I yet to tell thee;
would to God that thou lent thine ears and
thine understanding!

2. If thou desire to defend the Catholic
Faith, defend it above all by good works.

3. Thou must exalt My gifts in such wise,
as not to lose humility.

4. The faith that thou professest is My
gift; and the more thou praise it, the more
shouldst thou remember the bounty of My
grace.

5. No greater honour is there for a man,
than that of being admitted into the bosom
of My Church.

6. All the wealth of the world and all the
learning of men, what are they in comparison
with such an honour? Nothing.

7. Oh, if thou didst but comprehend the
excellence and profit of being a Christian,
the unbeliever would inspire thee with pity,
not with hatred.

8. If thou desire to teach one who knoweth

not the faith, the more learned he be, the more needful is it to begin with the simple alphabet.

9. If a man cling to error, do not argue vainly, do not insist; those truths that he acknowledgeth are the best beginning.

10. If thou bear high authority as a teacher, show by thine example the virtue which truth containeth.

11. Virtue and love are the two best weapons for destroying or discrediting error.

12. How can that doctrine be false which hath in its favour divine virtue?

13. How can that man be striving to deceive, who teacheth the truth, if he be ready to die for it with humility and meekness?

14. If thou desire to know truth from error, be master of thyself.

15. The more pure thou art, the more humbly thou live, the more wilt thou advance in the true way.

16. To know many things without holding true principles, is to dwell in a house without foundations and assailed by the winds.

17. Better is it to know little and live a holy life, than to possess much learning and to live in great wickedness.

18. Frivolity and vanity are the worst enemies of the Truth.

19. Pride and disordered self-love ever shield themselves behind error and deceit.

20. Truth is ever simple, ever standeth fast, never changeth; and the more it be attacked, the more it shineth forth.

21. Son, much virtue is needful to teach the ignorant; great stores of wisdom and humility are required to instruct the learned.

22. If thou stand on a firm foundation, learn much of human science ; all truths are akin : and learning is very useful in dealing with men and in winning them for God.

CHAPTER XX.

WHAT THE HEART OF MY MASTER CRIETH ALOUD.

1. Son, I desire that thou examine in My presence, not only against what faults and errors thou hast spoken, but also how many sins thou hast hindered by thy tact and My grace.

2. I desire that thou count up how often thou couldst have helped the good and hast not done so, and how often thou couldst have done good to those who have most

offended Me, and how much thou hast neglected this.

3. I desire that thou reckon how many labours thou hast undertaken in My service, and how many times thou hast manfully conquered thyself to please Me.

4. I desire that thou see in how many ways thou hast thwarted the conversion of sinners, and in what manner thou hast hindered the governing power of My Church.

5. I desire that thou tell Me why thou boastest of thy courage, when thou art not prudent ; why thou dost esteem thyself of consequence, when thou hast no power.

6. I desire that thou decide if thy conduct in church be profane or devout, and if thy life in the world be pagan or christian.

7. I desire that thou for once recount to Me what have been up till now the fruits of thy piety and religion, and how far thy devotion to devotions and thy want of self-renunciation have impeded thee.

8. I desire to hear from thy lips how many converts thy words and thy deeds have won, and how many souls thou hast made better by thy dealing with them, and by the perfect fulfilment of thine office.

9. If sinners and reprobates are less

worthy of blame than thou, in private or in public, inwardly or outwardly, do not deem thyself a sincere and fervent Catholic who hath practical influence, but rather a sinful and imperfect man who exposeth to danger the good name of My Cause.

10. How many are called to My reward! but how few set themselves to merit it!

11. And tell Me, My son, what wrong have I done unto thee, I, Whom thou often treatest so ill?

CHAPTER XXI.

HOW, BY ATTENDING TO CERTAIN THINGS,
I CAN FIT MYSELF FOR SUCCESS.

1. Son, bad principles and serious errors easily produce most serious consequences.

2. To embrace principles which are false or perverse, and not to fear the consequences, is nothing but folly.

3. To defend evil in principles, and to deny their natural consequences, is the action of him who would be a tyrant, and would make others his victims.

4. Light errors, if they spread freely, quickly become grave.

5. To permit that errors should grow freely and to pretend to aim at true liberty, is to desire that either thou thyself, or others may be deceived.

6. He who serveth a tyrant, will be the first to feel the whole weight of his hands.

7. He who eateth bad food, nourisheth sickness.

8. He who cannot distinguish between error and truth, will be paid for his labour in false coin.

9. Son, be not deceived by appearances, nor be seduced by fair words.

10. Error beginneth by feigning to stand well with the truth; presently it raileth at her, as an evil. And when a lie triumpheth, it will persecute truth as an enemy.

11. It is better to know little, and not to be the slave of error, than to know much and to be deceived at every step.

12. He who holdeth fast to sound principles, will not fall into great errors.

13. He who hath not definite convictions, mistaketh great lies for truth.

14. He who aimeth at deceit, is lavish of promises; he who would lead astray, is swift to flatter.

15. If thou desire not to fall into dangerous errors, seek counsel from those better than thyself.

16. If thou desire to attain the Truth, study much: if thou desire to defend it, confer with many others.

17. Be not dazzled by glittering brilliance, nor shaken by vain novelties.

18. False progress lendeth a helping hand to the worst back-slider.

19. The more evil be civilized, the more is it insidious and refined.

20. If progress be entirely in outward things, little by little both temporal and eternal good will be lost.

21. Son, if thou desire to know many things, do not forget to learn those which are of consequence to thyself.

22. Make thyself fit to do good, and thou shalt reap many goods.

23. First acquire great virtues, and later thou shalt realize thy projects.

CHAPTER XXII.

OF SOME COUNSELS THAT WILL SERVE ME IN MY SOCIAL WORK.

1. My son, many there are who desire that I should love them, but few who devote themselves to serving Me.

2. Many there are who desire that I should give them rewards, but few who offer Me sacrifices.

3. Many there are who honour Me when they feel the approval of the world, but few who come forward to defend Me when men despise Me.

4. Many there are who wish to share My glory, but few who practise My virtues.

5. How many desire to be respected, and Heaven contemneth them.

6. How many desire the honours of the world, and Virtue laugheth them to scorn.

7. How many desire the esteem of men, and they are persecutors of the poor.

8. How many desire to live without a thought of Heaven, and Death lieth in wait for them.

9. How very many offer themselves as guides of the multitude, and they themselves walk in the way of iniquity.

10. If thou desire to labour for the sake of men, it is necessary that thou be intent on learning how to reach the inmost depths of the human heart.

11. When a man is alone, then what is within him appeareth outwardly.

12. When he hath opportunity to act, then his inclinations are revealed.

13. When he enjoyeth his pleasures, then his vices are made manifest.

14. When he seeth without being seen, then he regardeth that after which he lusteth.

15. When he is carried away by anger, then he speaketh of that which he desireth.

16. Trust not to vain appearances, nor to manifold offers of service.

17. Despise no man because of his sins and imperfections.

18. If thou see sins committed, provide the surest remedy.

19. When a physician hath succeeded in finding the disease, he reneweth his confidence; and, the more he knoweth how to fulfil his duty, the more he loveth the patient, even though the malady arise from the fault of the sick man. All his aversion will be towards the malady, and he will use the knife without injury to the sufferer.

CHAPTER XXIII.

OF THE QUALITIES OF TRUE ZEAL.

1. In the city of pride, My son, they committed much and very great injustice against their neighbour.

2. And three zealous men desired to prevent these great injuries.

3. And the first was very impetuous, and began by denouncing the wickedness of the most unjust and powerful of the proud.

4. And the sinner became enraged and made himself still more unjust and arrogant.

5. The second then came forward, very humble and peaceable; but in dealing with the proud, he recoiled from them as from a people already lost and incorrigible.

6. And the proud, seeing his fear, made a mock of him. And they persisted in their iniquities in the sight of God and man.

7. Then said the most learned of the three: this is an enterprize for me. And he went to the proud and made a discourse to them, very learned and eloquent, which they did not heed.

8. And the vanity and presumption of the haughty ones increased, and one of them in his turn, in an arrogant discourse, made a like display of his learning.

9. And the many ignorant extolled him, and held it a very glorious thing to sin much.

10. But one man, compassionate and virtuous, who had himself once been very arrogant, judged rightly that pride was the

most terrible evil which could afflict his brother, and he prayed to God in humility of heart for the proud.

11. And by the example he gave them of virtue, and by the profitable services he rendered them, he prevented much evil, and was regarded in the city as a good man and an excellent citizen.

12. And little by little he gained the affection of the proud, and at the same time, with much gentleness and discretion, he instructed and converted them.

13. And it happened many times that the proud began to commit fewer evil deeds, so as not to offend so loyal a friend. And thereafter, being now better disposed, they perceived the beauty of virtue, and the fitness and justice of the divine commandments and the truth of the Church's teaching. And at last they held it a worthy and a profitable thing to submit, as in fact they did submit, to the influence of grace.

14. And he became very popular and esteemed for his services and attentions to others, and was regarded by all as a man truly Christian.

15. And in truth I tell thee that thenceforth less sins were committed.

16. And even the most depraved and

wicked did not dare to lie against God as they had been wont.

17. But there were other servants of My Father who dwelt in that same city. And when they saw some proud man that was not fully converted, or who, when just converted, did not begin to give signs of humility in an heroic degree, then did they affront him publicly.

18. And they spoke thus: "Let us go and cast in his teeth his former wickedness: none shall be allowed to pervert."

19. And they did this many times, and without availing themselves of other means for the good of the poor sinners.

20. And to avoid the danger of deceit and error, they fell into many errors.

21. And to guard the humility of the humble, they cast back the proud on their wickedness.

22. And yet, in truth I tell thee, he doth more, who converteth a sinner of a hundred years, than he who preserveth in their innocence a hundred children.

23. And he doth more for the Truth who converteth one evil-doer, than he who only contenteth himself with convicting a hundred false teachers of lying.

24. And again, if it be needful to guard

thyself and others from the perils of the false and cunning, it is also of the greatest profit for the good of the simple and the humble themselves, to convert sinners of power and influence.

25. In very truth, I tell thee, those servants so wanting in wisdom and discretion, with their offensive and persistent tactics, were not able to prevent the evils which come from false conversions and from the cunning of perverse deceivers.

26. And never did they convert one of the proud ;

27. Nor did they make the good more humble.

28. For against the evil of pride it is necessary to oppose the virtue of true humility;

29. And against hatred, the self-sacrificing tenderness of a love all divine;

30. And against deceit, prudence ;

31. And with the lion's strength for the struggle when that be needed, it is most fitting that thou join the sweetness of honey for attracting.

32. And My son, the good work consisteth not in much speaking, nor in toil, but in having great charity and in knowing how to labour with humility of heart.

CHAPTER XXIV.

HOW I MUST RENOUNCE MYSELF, IF I WOULD BECOME PROFITABLE.

1. If thou desire to do anything of profit for Me, aim at leaving thyself.

2. I left My Father to redeem the slaves, I left My Mother to do good to My brethren. I left Nazareth to teach My disciples : I left Jerusalem to die for My very enemies.

3. If thou leave thy self-love, I will open to thee very wide horizons.

4. Thou wilt learn little if thou always think of thyself.

5. Thou wilt have little success unless thou study the triumphs and progress of the wicked.

6. Thou wilt acquire little unless thou succeed in loving renunciation.

7. If thou wait that others should seek thee, thou wilt wait long before meeting a good helper and a good friend.

CHAPTER XXV.

A SUMMARY OF THINGS I MUST NEVER FORGET.

1. Son, if thou know not how to conquer thyself, how wilt thou make thyself superior to Death?

2. If thou have no inward strength, what canst thou do outwardly?

3. If thou possess not deep convictions, what will all thine arguments avail?

4. If thou know not how to keep silence, how wilt thou succeed in speaking?

5. If thou have not an active spirit, who will wish to go with thee?

6. If thou have not strength of mind, what will be the power of thy will?

7. Mould thyself to-day; examine thyself; learn to know thyself; repress thyself, and make thyself truly a man and fully a master of thine impulses.

8. The man who hath not a true knowledge of himself, only becometh a stumbling-block.

9. The man who cannot restrain himself, will be capable of doing more harm to the good than the worst of enemies.

10. If that which thou sayest or dost tend to lessen the power of authority, more profitable will it be for thee to do nothing and be silent.

CHAPTER XXVI.

A CANTICLE WHICH INSPIRETH ME TO IMITATE THE DIVINE MASTER.

1. To-day, beloved son, will I teach thee that triumphant song of Hope, re-echoing from groans and sighs, and inspired by the Truth, which consoleth in exile those who live for Heaven.

2. Rejoice, ye poor,
   For He Who was so poor amongst men,
   The Man-God, the Saviour, Life Eternal,
   And the Everlasting Bliss of the lowly,
   Jesus Christ, is your God.

3. Rejoice, ye humble,
   For He Who was so meek of heart,
   The Man-God, the Saviour, Life Eternal,
   And the Everlasting Bliss of the lowly,
   Jesus Christ, is your God.

4. Rejoice, ye sick,
   For He Who knew so much sorrow,

The Man-God, the Saviour, Life Eternal,
And the Everlasting Bliss of the lowly,
Jesus Christ, is your God.

5. Rejoice, ye weary,
   For He Who laboured all His life,
   The Man-God, the Saviour, Life Eternal,
   And the Everlasting Bliss of the lowly,
   Jesus Christ, is your God.

6. Rejoice, ye desolate,
   For He Who drained the chalice of
       bitterness,
   The Man-God, the Saviour, Life Eternal,
   And the Everlasting Bliss of the lowly,
   Jesus Christ, is your God.

7. Rejoice, ye calumniated,
   For He Who was accused of so many
       crimes,
   The Man-God, the Saviour, Life Eternal,
   And the Everlasting Bliss of the lowly,
   Jesus Christ, is your God.

8. Rejoice, ye despised,
   For He Who was deemed the most
       abject of men,
   The Man-God, the Saviour, Life Eternal,
   And the Everlasting Bliss of the lowly,
   Jesus Christ, is your God.

9. Rejoice, ye disgraced,
   For He Who was placed below Barabbas,
   The Man-God, the Saviour, Life Eternal,

And the Everlasting Bliss of the lowly,
Jesus Christ, is your God.

10. Rejoice, ye persecuted,
For He Who was so cruelly used by all,
The Man-God, the Saviour, Life Eternal,
And the Everlasting Bliss of the lowly,
Jesus Christ, is your God.

11. Rejoice, ye defenceless,
For He who died forsaken on the Cross,
The Man-God, the Saviour, Life Eternal,
And the Everlasting Bliss of the lowly,
Jesus Christ, is your God.

12. Rejoice, ye multitudes,
If ye love the Faith, if ye are in grace :
For, through Jesus Christ, the Man-
God, the Saviour, Life Eternal,
And the Everlasting Bliss of the lowly,
Yours is the kingdom of Heaven.

13. Rejoice always in your God, rejoice in
your spirit, for, if ye love purity, if
ye walk in the truth, if ye are not
blinded by vanity, if ye are not
seduced by deceitful pleasures nor
disturbed by passion ; if ye are faithful, if ye are good, then
Yours is the kingdom of Heaven.

14. Pray, labour ; serve God in perpetual
submission to His Divine Providence ;
live, all united by charity, and always

brethren in the one, true, Holy Catholic Church, and rejoice without ceasing, for God our Lord, Jesus Christ, is ever Just, is ever Good, the Consolation of those who suffer and hope, the eternal Reward of all the lowly and lovers of peace.

To Him, together with the Father and the Holy Ghost, three distinct Persons and One True God, be glory for ever and ever. Amen.

BOOK THE SECOND.

Fac Bonum—" Do Good."

Psalm xxxiii. 15.

CHAPTER I.

OF THE GREAT CHARITY WHICH I MUST HAVE TO BE A PROFITABLE MAN.

1. My son, love the Faith much, for without Faith it is impossible that thou canst believe in Me in a fitting and secure manner.

2. But believe much in the virtue which Charity possesseth for doing all with great fidelity and for transforming all.

3. The miracles of Faith were revealed to the world, and the world remained enlightened.

4. Ages ago the miracles of hope were manifested to the ages, and the ages became civilized.

5. To-day and to-morrow the foresight and sacrifices of Charity will prevent many evils and will save society.

6. Have much faith in the Charity which is grounded on Hope and on Faith, and I say to thee that thou shalt see marvels.

7. Charity is very wide; Charity is very deep.

8. Charity raiseth itself very high; Charity abaseth itself very low.

9. Charity is very strong; Charity is very gentle.

10. Charity giveth light; Charity giveth foresight.

11. Charity is very silent; Charity speaketh very loudly.

12. Charity saveth the good; Charity sacrificeth itself.

13. Charity always toileth; Charity always suffereth.

14. Charity worketh miracles; Charity blunteth errors and killeth vices.

15. If thou have much Faith, thou shalt move mountains; if thou have great Charity, thou shalt draw men.

16. Charity is so great, that only in My Church canst thou find it.

17. Without riches, it possesseth treasures; without study, it knoweth very much; without guile, it is prudent; without seduction, it vanquisheth; without doing injury, it gaineth the mastery, and ministering to all, it is free.

18. He who hath great Charity, hath in himself the likeness and the throne of the eternal Trinity.

19. He who hath great Charity, shareth without doubt in My divinity.

20. He who is on fire with Charity, though

he be but humble and lowly, is king of himself before his fellow-men.

21. I have said: ye are gods, if ye love much and in very truth.

22. Two are the laws of love: "Thou shalt love the Lord thy God with thy whole heart, and with thy whole soul, and with thy whole mind, and with all thy strength. And thou shalt love thy neighbour as thyself," if thou hast Charity.

23. Thou must then love God above all, setting thy God above all.

24. Thou must love the Lord thy God with all thy powers, with all thy learning, with all thy science, with all thy riches, with all thine influence, with all thy dignities, with all thine undertakings.

25. Thou must love thy God more than all thine aims, more than all thy ways, more than all thine occupations, more than all thy friends, more than all thy surroundings, more than all thy happiness and comfort.

26. Thou must love thy God in all thy fears, in all thy desolation, in all thy desires, in all thy hopes, in all thy joys, in all thy sorrows, in all thy labours, in all thy rest, in all thy duties, in all thine honours, in all thy glories, in all thy glorious humiliations.

27. Thou must love thy God in the begin-

ning, thou must love Him in the middle, thou must love Him in the end, if thou desire to rejoice in Him for ever without end.

28. He who loveth his God, glorifieth Him; he who glorifieth his God, exalteth himself; and he who exalteth himself in God shall remain in glory eternally and for ever.

29. In Charity abideth the holiness of justice, of prudence, of fortitude, of temperance.

30. In Charity abideth rest and peace, and the realization of blessedness.

31. If thou have Charity and Charity make thee an apostle, thou wilt have the treasure of treasures, the science of sciences, the happiness of happiness, and thou wilt shine like the sun in its splendour.

32. The truest progress, the highest advancement, the most powerful force, the purest and greatest perfection cannot reach a higher dignity and position than to establish in man and in the world the kingdom and the laws of Charity.

33. Charity is the beginning of life, it is the moving force of life, it is the perfection of life, it is the living rest and eternal possession of happiness.

34. There is no progress without Charity,

there is no greatness without Charity, there is no dominion without Charity, there is no power without Charity, there is no sovereignty without Charity, and there is no true life, if it be not lived in Charity.

35. Charity is the strength of the feeble, the health of the sick, the consolation of the afflicted, the relief of those in need, the correction of the proud, the punishment of the wicked and the union of true brotherhood.

36. He who despiseth Faith, shall perish everlastingly; he who despiseth Charity, shall suffer everlastingly and shall not be able to love.

37. Oh, Charity, life of love, life of eternal blessedness: what happiness for man if he could find thee in Me!

38. My son, what happiness for thee if thou understand these things! But if thou desire to study these truths, then do good works.

CHAPTER II.

OF THE BLESSEDNESS AND SECURITY OF MY WAY.

1. Blessed are they who believe; for if they keep My commandments, they shall see My promises fulfilled in themselves.

2. Blessed are they who hope; for if they live according to the faith, they shall be reckoned amongst valiant Christians in My triumph.

3. Blessed are they who love; for if they fulfil their duty, they shall obtain the happiness of the truly faithful.

4. Blessed are the rich; for if they despise their wealth, they shall obtain the treasures of the poor of spirit.

5. Blessed are the learned; for if they put true virtues into practice, they shall obtain the reward of the lowly.

6. Blessed are the mighty; for if they favour the needy for My sake, they shall obtain eternal life.

7. Blessed are they who rule; for if they show forth in their actions the holiness of My precepts, they shall merit an eternal kingdom.

8. Blessed are they who submit to My Church; for if they confess Me before the world, I will be their portion for ever in Heaven.

9. No man cometh to My glory if he exalt not My name.

10. There is but one Faith; there is but one Baptism; there is but one Church; there is but one Saviour; there is but one Heaven; there is but one eternal God.

11. I am the Holiness of Justice; I am the Holiness of Truth.

12. He who cometh after Me hateth a lie; he who loveth My goodness, hateth iniquity.

CHAPTER III.

THAT I MUST GREATLY STRENGTHEN MY SOUL, IF I DESIRE TO BE PROFITABLE.

1. My son, he who hath much regard for himself and taketh little account of Me, shall make little progress.

2. The more thou forsake thyself, the more shalt thou find Me; the more thou seek thyself, the less part shalt thou have with Me.

3. If thou seek to enjoy My sweetness and consolation, and to know how good is fervour and the practice of virtue, give thyself up to a virtuous life and to works of fervour.

4. He who tasteth the delights of the spirit, esteemeth little the feasts and pastimes of this world.

5. Didst thou know how sweet it is to do good, and how profitable for thyself to teach others the way to Heaven, thou wouldst work after a very different manner.

6. What good hast thou effected, if thou hast done no good works?

7. What pleasure remaineth to thee from abandoning thyself to pleasures?

8. "Are ye also yet without understanding?" And yet how much dost thou think thyself to know in this life!

9. Seek goodness, and thou shalt find perfection.

10. Seek the profit of others, and thou shalt find rest.

11. Labour for My glory, and the light of noon-day shall shine in all thy works.

12. Alas, how few profit by the manifold means I have placed in their hands!

13. Alas, how few devote themselves to tending My vineyard!

14. I have called thee out of nothing that thou mightest offer Me the fruit of thy labours.

15. If thou hast heard My voice, hide not thyself from Me, nor answer Me with excuses.

16. I know what thou canst do; I ask not from thee more than is just.

17. Know that much will be asked from him to whom much hath been given.

18. Many there are who exclaim: "What can I do?" and foolishly answer: "I can do nothing."

19. Think on the evil thou hast committed, and thou wilt know what good thou hast to do.

20. Remember how far thy power of sinning hath carried thee, and thou wilt understand what thou canst do with My help.

21. I ask of thee nothing beyond what thou canst perform with My grace.

22. Do not accuse Me of weakness, for I am All-Powerful.

23. What will it profit thee to say: "My weakness is very great," if by so speaking thou foster thy sloth?

24. Oh, how subtle is inordinate self-love!

25. If thou desire to master thy self-love,

foster a great and holy love, a love that inspireth good works.

CHAPTER IV.

HOW I CAN BECOME USEFUL TO THE CAUSE.

1. My son, thou must know that, next to striving for thine eternal salvation, thou canst do nothing so pleasing to Me as to labour for My Cause.

2. But deceive not thyself, nor think that thou dost much for My glory and for the spreading of My saving influence, because thou hast done some one good thing and feelest very devout in thine exercises of piety.

3. As there are many mansions in Heaven, so are there many vocations on earth.

4. To those who are drawn to offer Me in a special manner the incense of their fervent and humble prayers, I show My will with manifest signs and call them for the good of the whole world.

5. But I prefer that others, without neglecting prayer and self-denial, intercede

by means of active effort and glorify Me in their outward work.

6. But alas, some, through littleness of spirit or absorption in self, abandon the social field of divine glory.

7. How long, ye children of light, will ye keep your eyes closed, and become victims by allowing Hell to conquer?

8. If I am the King of Kings, and the Lord of all who have dominion, why do ye not render that full homage due to Me from whom all dominion cometh?

9. In the beginning, the Church was completely filled by My faithful sons, and to-day, Christians all leave it in complete abandonment.

10. Deem not that thou renderest Me great service, unless thou fulfil thy duties better than the unbelievers.

11. By this shall men know you to be My faithful disciples, if ye become eminent in observing righteous laws.

12. If through humility thou shun positions of honour, make thyself worthy thereof by thy services.

13. If wickedness increase greatly, it will do more injury than death itself.

14. Cease not to be useful to My Cause, from fear of being praised.

15. Have a pure intention, since thou hast ever in thyself enough of baseness and confusion.

16. Cease not to influence public life through fear of opposition and of insult, for My Justice will be thine honour and thy defence.

17. How wouldst thou that the world praise and acknowledge Me, if unbelievers gain the victory?

18. The more thou rise with merit to high and profitable dignities, the better example of justice and humility wilt thou be able to give.

19. Have no regard for self in thy desires, nor cease to serve Me in thine undertakings.

20. The more thou sacrifice thyself for all without hesitation, the more wilt thou honour Me before the people, with thine oblations of justice and of praise.

CHAPTER V.

OF THE GREAT QUALITIES I MUST ACQUIRE,
IF I DESIRE TO BECOME A PRACTICAL
CATHOLIC.

1. Son, thou hast yet much to learn and much to practise, if thou desire to be of great profit.

2. Seek to make constant use of those lawful methods which, considering all the chances and circumstances, most conduce to a good result. This, My son, must be thy chief occupation, if thou desire to do much in a short time.

3. Strive also to cultivate to their highest degree thine energies, faculties and resources, in order to draw from them all the best possible effects. On this, My son, thou must insist firmly and constantly, if thou desire to be very profitable.

4. In the same way, in every action thou must apply thy forces in a manner most gentle, most firm, most prompt, most sure, least wasteful and most complete. This, My son, must be thy chief habit of mind, if thou aim at being really practical.

5. In every kind of enterprise chiefly fix

thine eyes on that part of it most easy and practicable, most suited to thy character, qualities and virtues, and least fraught with danger and injurious consequences. If thou do this, My son, thy prudence shall be very great and profitable.

6. Son, if it be necessary to reform, do not begin without asking if thou oughtest not to reform thyself.

7. If thou must destroy or initiate, do not begin by making much noise.

8. If thou hast to do great things, to undertake much labour, or to finish a thing with haste, despise as less than nothing thy punctilios of worldly honour.

9. If thou must vanquish by attraction, do not despise minute and insignificant details.

10. Son, very great must be thy discretion and thy judgment, if thou wouldst do or undo with profit in this world.

11. But before all, My son, it is fitting that thou attend to thine own state, to make thyself a most useful instrument of My grace, a man in reality a saint, deeply Christian and truly catholic, apostolic and Roman.

12. This, My son, must be thy greatest wisdom, if thou understand in thy heart what being wise signifieth.

13. Oh, what high thoughts and what ardent desires thou must have to be a great Catholic!

14. And how much thou must do in thyself to become actively profitable and profitably fruitful.

15. If thou seek to be very christian, thou must become very sincere, very humble and very charitable.

16. Unite thyself to Me and we will be true friends.

17. If thou seek to be very catholic, thou must become a very conscientious, very practical Christian, and on all sides and in all things, correspond very exactly with the holiness of My Church and with the true, lively profession of the Truth.

18. Labour with My grace, and I will make thee very fruitful.

19. If thou seek to be very apostolic, sacrifice in very truth thy petty, personal, earthly interests, in so far as they prevent thee from doing and suffering great things for the good name and prosperity of My Cause.

20. Son, the more thou give thyself to Me, the more canst thou do in union with Me.

21. Lastly, My son, if thou desire to be

on the side of My Vicar, thou must submit thy judgments and passions to his views and wishes, and not allow thyself to be overcome or misled by the personal influence of any man.

22. Then wilt thou be all Mine, when I can devote thee to My Vicar to be an active instrument in his service.

23. Thou wilt find much in My words, and thou wilt learn much, if thou ponder over them with a humble heart.

24. If thou do not oppose Me with inward resistance, nor forge for thyself outward impediments, I will make thee a great Catholic, whose influence and undertakings shall be most profitable for the saving of souls.

CHAPTER VI.

OF THE EFFICACY OF MY MASTER'S EXAMPLE.

1. My words are a great gift from Heaven: listen to them and thou wilt understand many truths.

2. Educate the people to virtue and truth, and thou wilt save society.

3. Where misery holdeth sway, hatred from Hell will prevail rather than love.

4. Labour for the masses; solace their needs, and they will acknowledge thy truths and thy virtues.

5. I have bestowed freedom on the slaves; I have restored to woman her greatness; I have granted life to infancy; I have ennobled poverty.

6. All My teaching is in favour of the lowly; all My glories I promise to the humble.

7. Therefore will the humble and the lowly love Me, and the mighty will adore Me.

8. I watch over all and over each one; I have united all in one body.

9. Jew and Gentile, civilized and savage, I have filled them with kindliness and brotherly love.

10. I have made of them one great family, where all might dwell in unity as children of My Father.

11. I have dispersed Mine Apostles throughout the whole world, so that they might sow the divine seed which bringeth forth in My disciples a hundred-fold.

12. I desire that every man should share in My greatness, and that all should be rich by grace as I am by nature.

13. I made Myself the lowest of all and the humblest of the people, so that none might esteem himself vile.

14. I came that I might restore glory to My Father, and for this I made Myself the slave of men and ministered to all.

15. I began by giving an example; so that all might learn, My disciples and the masters of My disciples.

16. I had respect unto the mighty, and I loved the lowly; I questioned the doctors, and I taught the ignorant.

17. I opened My mouth in loving-kindness, and I sat amongst the little ones.

18. If I have uttered hard words, they were directed against seeming virtues and against those who misused My gifts.

19. Those who taught error I refuted with their own arguments.

20. Woe to you who know the truth! Woe to you who can do good! Woe to you who have influence! For all these I shall ask of you a strict account.

CHAPTER VII.

HOW BY HUMILITY AND TRUTH I CAN LET MY LIGHT SHINE BEFORE MEN.

1. The children of light show forth their good works to give testimony of the light.

2. If thy works be good, glorify God thereby, and "enlighten them that sit in darkness and in the shadow of death."

3. What thou hast hath been given to thee for the good of many. Do not then quench the light of thy works.

4. Seek not to shine for thine own glory, but rather to exalt Him who enlighteneth the humble.

5. The more there shine forth in thee true humility, the greater will be the splendour of thy works.

6. If thou shine by thy learning, and thy learning shine not by thy faith, it may be that thou enlighten others, but thou wilt certainly thyself remain in darkness.

7. Of a truth, I tell thee, that it were better for the proud if they knew nothing, than that they should use their knowledge to injure the faith of the little ones, and to bring eternal perdition on themselves.

8. The learning of the vain dazzleth rather than enlighteneth.

9. The learning of the proud doth more injury to progress than the folly of fools.

10. Whereto doth science profit, if it aid not faith?

11. No humble soul hath been lost, but many are the wise men who have been led astray.

12. But if thou have learning and faith, thou art yet in danger: for I shall ask an exact account of the great gift given to thee.

13. There was one who sought to bury his talent, and he was condemned for it.

14. According to thy state of life, show forth the truth and the knowledge that is in thee, and thy name shall shine in the firmament.

15. If the heavens proclaim My glory, how much more should not thine intelligence proclaim it?

16. There is no man so unlettered that he may not teach others by practising the counsels of eternal Truth.

17. The word of a humble man is oft-times more profitable than all the fine speeches of one who trusteth in his eloquence.

18. If, however, thou know that I have

given thee the talent of an orator, forget not to place it at My service.

19. I am thy Master; for My glory have I created thee.

20. And if I desire to use My gifts that are in thee—forget not that they are such—thereby I confer on thee an immense benefit.

CHAPTER VIII.

OF THE DISCRETION I NEED TO BECOME A PROFITABLE MAN.

1. Son, to hold very safe principles is the best way of not losing time.

2. The more the lower classes are taught, the greater share will they have in the destiny of the peoples.

3. The more thou devote thyself to the poor and simple, the more profit wilt thou obtain for the good of the nations.

4. Seek not to remain permanently in one position, for otherwise thou wilt not advance in any direction.

5. When a change can do much good or

much harm, it is necessary not to leave it in the power of the enemy.

6. Some only see what they hold before their eyes; others never tire in thinking of what remaineth behind their backs.

7. If present things absorb thee without measure, how wilt thou provide against great evils to come?

8. How will it serve thee to dwell night and day on the past, since thou canst not amend it?

9. How will it serve thee to sing the praises of other days, if it only help thee to be always weeping?

10. If thou expend all thine energies in combating one person, when wilt thou undertake the really good works?

11. If thou canst not begin anything till all submit to thy judgment, instead of doing great deeds, thou wilt reap many disputes.

12. If all were just and perfect, how wouldst thou obtain the fruits of patience?

13. Boast not of being courageous or upright; it is enough that thou be so in truth.

14. The greater the defects thou hast learned to bear with, the more easily wilt thou be able to remedy them.

15. If thou cherish very perfect ideals, begin by combating thine own failings.

16. If thou canst do great things, do not fire off thine artillery against a gnat.

17. If thou always meet with difficulties in thine affairs, scrutinize closely thy thoughts.

18. If thou canst not conquer an aversion, do not think thyself great, for thy heart is very little.

19. Listen, My son: thou wilt do more by submitting to others and serving them, than by seeking to be their leader.

20. Men will believe thee very great when they see thee able to conquer thyself by strength of character.

21. If thou listen to My counsels and put them into practice, thou shalt understand high truths concerning the destinies of nations.

22. Many are useless instruments, because they are caught in the nets which they themselves have made.

23. Lift up thine eyes; contemplate what is great; fix thy desires on the most noble enterprises; and then undertake only those that are most profitable and feasible.

24. If thou make not imaginary foes, nor engage in lost battles, thou wilt win many friends.

CHAPTER IX.

OF THE GREAT COURAGE WHICH I REQUIRE
IN ORDER TO SUCCEED IN MINE UNDER-
TAKINGS.

1. Son, the more evil the times, the greater must be thy courage.

2. If thou have confidence in Me, thou wilt have no fear for the good success of thine undertakings.

3. What courage should not a man possess, when he hath God on his side !

4. Cast, then, from thy spirit all affliction and fear; they are the outcome of thy cowardice and the action of thine enemy.

5. If thine enemies have not yet conquered, why art thou willing to give them the victory by thy faint-heartedness ?

6. The fervent Christian laboureth the more, when his labour is more needed and more for My glory.

7. If thou do as much as thou art able with My grace, then hast thou already conquered, and I hold in My hands thy crown of victory.

8. I do not insist that thou triumph over

Mine enemies; but thou must do thine utmost.

9. Although thou do not gain a visible and transitory victory over the wicked, thou dost already conquer if thou bear thyself as a valiant soldier.

10. Oh, how many things thou understandest not as yet, and how very narrow is thy heart!

11. To correspond to My designs is to conquer.

12. To work for My glory with all thy force is to conquer.

13. To make thyself superior to thy weariness is to conquer.

14. To persevere in thine enterprise in spite of the suggestions of the devil is to conquer.

15. To look to My power for victory, when thou hast done all that thy hand findeth to do, is to conquer.

CHAPTER X.

HOW THROUGH CHARITY, I SHALL LAY HOLD OF GREAT IDEALS.

1. Son, the cause for which I desire thee to labour is no mean or paltry one, but highly exalted and most noble.

2. Look then no longer on lower things, but rather lift thine eyes to the higher, and hope not for good results through unworthy methods, however powerful they seem, nor through merely human efforts, however mighty they be.

3. In Me dwelleth a virtue above all virtue ; in Me is an efficacy above all efficacy.

4. All carnal pride shall suffer pain ; all malevolence shall be overcome ; all satire shall be silenced ; and all anger shall burn to its own destruction.

5. The triumphs that are gained against Me now, are the forerunners and figures of My own triumph in eternity.

6. I shall triumph over evil, I shall triumph over injustice, I shall triumph over error ; I shall triumph over concupiscence and vice.

7. All will be eternally subject unto Me, and will for ever proclaim My Holiness, My Wisdom, and My Power, My Bounty and Mine infinite Charity.

8. Even as the rebel angels proclaim the virtue and equity of My Justice, so shall the mighty of this world likewise proclaim, willingly or unwillingly, the immensity of My divine Love, and of Mine infinite Goodness and Mercy.

9. Work with uprightness and sanctity, and do for My glory what thou understandest, if indeed thou understand these things.

10. Despise not human and earthly means, for all good proceedeth from God, and is for the praise and glory of thy God.

11. Strive to render good that which is indifferent, and to render holy that which is good, and to convert that which is holy to the temporal advantage and spiritual profit of men.

12. I have created the whole visible world for the good of human creatures and for the glory of My Name.

13. Much yet remaineth for thee to do, if thou desire to correspond with My grace.

14. My apostles triumphed over the world especially by Faith ; those who suffered

martyrdom triumphed over the devil chiefly by Hope; the Christians of to-day will obtain a glorious triumph over the flesh by Charity.

15. Reflect then how much thou must love sacrifice, and how much thou must labour for love.

16. The more widespread thy benevolence and good works, the more fruitful will be thy victories.

17. Ah, if thou wert but holy and didst love many, thou wouldst marvel to see the profit and glory of thy triumphs.

18. Then couldst thou promote the general manifestation of moral victories, then couldst thou keep the festival of My sweet love; then wouldst thou relish the true yearly celebration of My inexhaustible mercies; then wouldst thou place before the world the glorious works of My Church and of My Saints, whereby I teach men the ideal of love and of glory.

19. And if this appeareth too great for thee, take heed that thou art not unfaithful in little things, for I will judge thee according to thy works.

CHAPTER XI.

THAT ALL CONSTRAINETH ME TO BE **VERY** COMPASSIONATE.

1. What doth it serve thee to possess what thou hast, if thy soul lack the true good?

2. It is a great thing to benefit men's bodies, but far more profit wilt thou find in helping their souls.

3. If thy treasures profit thee not for Heaven and for growth in virtue, thou wilt be as a barren tree, with many leaves but without fruit.

4. Behold how many are drawn into error by the deceits of the wicked; how many believe lies, because they know not the teaching of truth.

5. Oh, how hard a heart thou hast, if so many evils do not move thee!

6. With what difficulty shalt thou enter the gate of Heaven, if thou carry such a weight on the wings of thy soul.

7. The poor complain of My providence, but thou shalt answer for their complaints.

8. The activity of the good is seen to

fail, but it is to thee that this weakness shall be imputed.

9. And alas for thee, if these facts are distasteful to thee, and if with unmeasured extravagance thou encourage luxury!

10. It is good that each man live conformably to his station, but he who is richer ought to show himself more generous and ready to give.

11. He who will not give for My Cause, to whom doth he give for love of Me?

12. And he who giveth not for love of Me, whom doth he honour?

13. Every good action tendeth to glory and praise. Whom dost thou glorify and praise by thine actions?

14. Oh, unprofitable servant, if thou regardest thyself, and dost not serve Me! Oh, barren tree, if thou bringest forth no fruit for Me!

15. My first faithful disciples laid their riches at the feet of the Apostles. And thou dost not wish to give of thy superfluities for the most holy of apostolates.

16. I dwell in each of the poor; all that he receiveth at thy hand, it is I that receive it.

17. If thou give for bodily food, it is good and oft-times necessary.

18. If thou give for spiritual life, it is better and well-nigh always more useful.

19. If there are rich gluttons and wretched paupers, it is because the world rejecteth My teaching.

20. The well-being of the soul often dependeth upon sufficiency not failing to the body.

21. And the health of the body dependeth very much upon the virtues of the soul.

22. I watch for all, and I forget nothing.

23. Where two shall unite in My Name to do good to many poor, there am I as a loving Father.

24. Where three practise virtue for the good of many rich, there am I as a king upon his throne.

25. But where many labour for great and small, for the temporal and eternal good of My Cause, there do I find My delight and My glory.

26. Oh, if thou didst love eternal treasures as thou desirest perishable ones, what homage wouldst thou not render Me on earth and what glory wouldst thou not receive in Heaven!

CHAPTER XII.

OF THE COUNSELS I MUST OBSERVE, IF I
DESIRE TO BECOME A PRACTICAL MAN.

1. Son, I will judge and reward thee according to thy works, and thou shalt obtain Mercy if thou have shown mercy.

2. Thou shalt enjoy the possession of the Truth, if thou have given alms of truth.

3. Thou shalt enjoy an eternal reward, if thou have given alms of good counsel.

4. Thou shalt enjoy the Sovereign Good, if thou have given alms of the true good.

5. Thou shalt enjoy unchanging peace in glory, if thou have given alms of useful correction.

6. One prudent counsel is of more avail than a three-fold alms in money.

7. The teaching of one good book hath more power than ten men armed and appointed to defend the right.

8. To co-operate for the well-being of the State doth more than to write marvels by the thousand.

9. If the laws are bad, the cities will be worse.

10. If evil be wrought by way of instruction, its effects will be the worse.

11. If it be impossible to build up, it will be the more difficult to destroy.

12. If there be no chance of doing good, who will be able to bear the evil?

13. To have much and not to do much, is to subject oneself to many obstacles.

14. Make thyself all things to all men, in order to make them better.

15. Be a magnet and seek the iron, and lose not thy power of attraction.

16. If the shepherd be clothed with a sheepskin, the lambs will follow him willingly.

17. But if he make himself a ravening wolf, he will be left without a flock.

18. He who permitteth and doth not prevent ill-doing, shall lose his life and his possessions.

19. And he who thinketh not of the salvation of souls, how will their prayers avail him at the hour of death?

CHAPTER XIII.

OF THE THINGS I MUST DO, IF I DESIRE TO BE A PRACTICAL MAN.

1. My son, if thou always dwell in the region of ideals, however excellent they may be, thou wilt never arrive at deeds.

2. If thou always restrict thyself to principles, when wilt thou draw practical conclusions from them?

3. Thou must seek the truth in such a way that thou forget not to study how thou canst put it into practice.

4. Oft-times those less learned and clever than others, are more prudent and useful.

5. Doctrine must be good and very pure, but likewise very fruitful.

6. Some would defend the Truth, and yet they know not how to defend and also to practise it.

7. Greater is the value of one good work than of a thousand empty discussions.

8. He who defendeth the Truth with good works, pleaseth Me more than he who engageth in defending truths with arguments by the thousand.

9. Expound the truth of My doctrine, and show forth its holiness in thy life.

10. My Truth is pure; My Truth is chaste; My Truth is humble; My Truth is charitable and fruitful.

11. What can be said against a mystery which hath on its side great virtues?

12. What can be said against a dogma which hath on its side practical self-denial by good works?

13. The practical man doth not stumble over his own arguments.

14. The practical man will not defend the Truth for the mere satisfaction of being seen to defend it.

15. The practical man is he who sayeth what will most conduce to action.

16. The wicked teach in such a manner, that at the same time they pervert.

17. Thou must teach in such a manner, as at the same time to convert and to direct.

18. Thou wilt profit more from a truth once deeply pondered over, than if it be praised a thousand times.

19. To be practical, thou must know well how to defend and also how to suffer.

20. To be practical, thou must know well how to speak and also how to be silent.

21. To be practical, thou must know well how to dispute and also how to convert.

22. To be practical, thou must know well how to attack and also how to excuse.

23. Men lose all the fruit, through a wrong way of putting a subject before others.

24. If thou art always out of season, how wilt thou be instant for good in season?

25. The unbeliever loveth a scandal: see that thou give him not this pleasure.

26. If certain errors have persisted long, it is because of the notoriety gained by their wicked authors.

27. Ask of Me success and sound judgment, and I will answer thee: "Be very humble."

28. A system of action must be preferred, just so far as it leadeth to success.

29. A particular good must be insisted on, just so far as it be not opposed to a more necessary and universal good.

30. If thou be a man of action, examine thy deeds; if thou be a man of dreams, examine in My presence thine omissions.

CHAPTER XIV.

HOW I CAN EASILY BENEFIT MYSELF AND OTHERS.

1. My son, if I have placed thee in a high position, see what thou owest to those below thee.

2. Thy very talents, thy gifts, thy wealth, are but so many proofs of My bounty.

3. The personal good of each ought to tend likewise to the benefit of the whole body.

4. As the hands serve the feet, so the feet also must help the hands.

5. There is none so lowly and of so little account that he cannot confer benefits.

6. When I have been, and am so generous to thee, canst thou show thyself niggardly towards Me?

7. So great a reward as attaining to eternal glory demandeth many tasks on earth.

8. Those who concern themselves for all, shall receive special favours from My Heart.

9. If thou desire to keep thy wealth securely, use it to help the most destitute.

10. And understand what I say not of material profit alone, but even more of that which concerneth moral and supernatural good.

11. Teach moderation to him who wasteth all.

12. Teach thrift to him who thinketh not of the morrow.

13. Teach an orderly life to him who liveth in disorder.

14. Teach care of his soul to him who corrupteth his body.

15. Teach rational conduct to him who liveth dissolutely.

16. Teach self-restraint to him who is carried away by passion.

17. Teach self-correction to him who only thinketh of acquiring knowledge.

18. Teach him how to die who knoweth not how to live.

CHAPTER XV.

OF THE WAY TO ACQUIRE TRUE GAINS.

1. My son, the powerful weapons thou must employ in the combat against error and wickedness must not come from the devil or the flesh, but must be very pure and spiritual.

2. In enterprises for the defence or furtherance of good, all profit dependeth upon My grace.

3. The more closely thou be united to Me, and the more humbly thou confide in the power of My arm, the greater shall be thy work, the more stable and profitable its result.

4. What thou canst not obtain by action, thou shalt obtain by prayer.

5. Very pleasing to Me is fervent supplication, when it is allied to the practice of constant diligence.

6. But if thou canst not join in the practice of external works, pray much for them with inner fervour.

7. If thy powers be little, work much; if they are great, do not omit any good in thy power.

8. Watch over My Cause with a pure intention, and I will watch over thine affairs.

9. Thou must not, however, neglect thine own affairs through idleness, for men will call thee, not a Catholic, but a fool.

10. Nevertheless, if I will that thou lose thy gains, accept from My hand the hidden blessing I give thee thereby.

11. Only to him who overcometh with Me, will I give the victory.

12. Him will I love and exalt who loveth and glorifieth Me.

13. If thou attend to the eternal Good, thou wilt know how to employ earthly goods for Heaven.

14. Tell Me: if thou possess virtues, where are thy good works?

15. Tell Me: if thou bargain with My Church, what love hast thou for thy soul?

16. Tell Me: if thou despise prayer, in what dost thou place thy trust?

17. One pure soul profiteth the world more than a million impure, however mighty.

18. One holy soul profiteth mankind more by a life of penance, than a million conceited orators.

19. Nevertheless, thou must not leave under control of the enemy any profitable and lawful method of action, for thou

dwellest in the world of men, not in the heaven of angels.

20. Commence thy work in humble prayer; continue to labour in humility and prayer; and thou must not omit at the end to pray humbly, with humility of heart.

21. Nothing is so fruitful on earth as true humility. It draweth down graces from Heaven and Me Myself with them.

22. With prayer, humility and chastity, thou wilt be able to labour and strive; without these virtues, thou mayest perchance make an impression, but thou wilt bear no fruit.

CHAPTER XVI.

OF THE PRUDENCE AND ENERGY NEEDED FOR MY WORK.

1. Many form innumerable projects, and they live without plan and without good order.

2. Better would it be for them to set before themselves the most urgent and necessary work, than to go about in discouragement through not fulfilling any resolution.

3. See to-day what thou hast to do for My Cause, and concentrate thine energies on carrying out thy determination.

4. If thou labour only on violent impulse, thou wilt be as the summer storm.

5. It is not torrents of rain nor flashes of frequent lightning which fertilise the fields.

6. Determined application and constant prudence can do more than all the exertions of a giant.

7. If the social soil be not fitly prepared, how wouldst thou that the seed should bring forth fruit in due season?

8. I began with a few, and these few laboured amongst many.

9. I showed them the whole earth, as the field for their constant toil; and to the end I Myself did not cease to labour in one small portion of My vineyard.

10. My Apostles likewise divided their task, and each traded with his own talents.

11. If thou desire miracles and marvellous triumphs, do thy duty as well as thou art able with My grace.

12. If thou do all that thou canst do, thou dost and desirest enough.

13. Distress not thyself in vain, if the victory be not yet attained.

14. He who breaketh the sod, he who plougheth the furrow, he who soweth and looketh to Heaven, meriteth from God a fitting increase.

15. Already the season for fruit is approaching, and thou, if thou be faithful, shalt enjoy the harvest at My table.

16. How wouldst thou, My son, that all should fall out according to thy desires, if thy desires are so changeable?

17. My son, why longest thou to see already the beauty of the harvest, if as yet thou have not laboured sufficiently?

18. Labour from this day forth; labour with method; labour on a fixed plan, and for that love of the work My grace inspireth.

19. Be very constant and brave, if thou desire to be a man, if thou desire to be a Christian.

20. Be very sensible, be very reasonable, if thou desire to live as a Catholic with true supernatural faith.

CHAPTER XVII.

HOW MUCH I MUST DO TO BRING HELP TO SOULS.

1. Thou art already satisfied, My son; already it seemeth to thee that thou hast accomplished much.

2. Assuredly, if thy works witness to thy virtues, and thy virtues commend thy works, take part in the joy of the saints, for thy name is already written in the Kingdom of Heaven.

3. The true servant never sayeth that he hath done enough, for he doth not seek his own ease, but the glory of God.

4. He writeth or he speaketh; he promoteth or perfecteth a work; he meditateth a new scheme, or he joineth in the undertakings of others; never doth he think of himself, save to obtain greater mastery over his passions, and to sacrifice himself with more purity and perfection.

5. The more thou hast done for Me, the more shouldst thou mistrust thyself.

6. Neither yield nor vainly fear: I am the strength of those who trust in Me.

7. Pray, labour, conquer, glorify and exalt

the Church; all this the Catholic oweth to the world.

8. If thou raise thine eyes on high, thou wilt see that God deserveth much more than thou dost; if thou turn thine eyes below, thou wilt see that it is but little thou hast done for thy neighbour.

9. I have created thee out of nothing to make thee the instrument of My glory.

10. I have drawn thee out of the abyss to make thee love thy brother.

11. I have united thee to My mystical Body, to make thee a useful member.

12. I have laid up an eternal joy for thee, if thou show thyself generous in this world.

13. When thou shalt have hindered a sin or brought a sinner to the way of conversion, then indeed mayest thou rejoice; of a very truth thou hast glorified the Lord, and thou hast not received thy soul in vain.

CHAPTER XVIII.

THAT I HAVE NO CAUSE FOR FEAR, IF I CLING TO CHRIST.

1. This is the day of victory and triumph; this is the day of thy glory.

2. If I will that thou live, thou wilt live; and if I will that thou die, thou wilt yet live.

3. The fury of the sea is now unchained; and the winds rage fiercely.

4. Why dost thou fear? Wherefore art thou terrified? Thine hour for martyrdom hath not yet come.

5. I am at thy side. If I seem to thee to slumber, be not troubled.

6. I am there with My word of power, and ready to put forth that power, to give thee victory.

7. I am He who commandeth the fury of the winds and of the sea. I am He that giveth the crown to him that overcometh.

8. Whether thou escape with life from the fight, or thou enter by death into My kingdom, it is for thee to conquer, if thou trust in My grace.

9. If at the feet of My minister thou hast burnt up thy sins, as a holocaust in the fire of charity, there is little that thine enemy can do.

10. If he can do aught, what is it, but what I permit?

11. Thou art Mine, thou art of the number of Mine elect.

12. Not so much as a hair of thy head shall be hurt by the rage of thine adversaries, of the opponents of thy faith and of My glory, if I do not desire it.

13. Confess Me then as a good knight of Christ, and as a noble son of thy country.

14. I will set majesty in thine aspect, serenity on thy brow, words of praise in thy mouth and the fire of charity in thy breast.

15. If thou art worthy to die for the Faith, thou shalt live eternally.

16. Go forth, then, armed with the power of the Cross, and blush not to confess Me as God before men.

17. If for Mine honour thou art insulted, of a certainty thou canst hope for no greater praise from the wicked.

18. Nor can greater glory befall a man in this world, than to die for God's glory while forgiving his enemies.

19. And only he who fighteth according to My laws, shall win an eternal crown.

20. I Myself will be thy reward, great above all greatness.

CHAPTER XIX.

IN HOW MANY WAYS I MAY BE UTTERLY CONFOUNDED, IF I AM NOT VERY COURAGEOUS.

1. Think not to do great good for My Name, if thou be not ready to endure much evil.

2. He who refuseth to suffer, or who is distressed beyond measure by pain, will readily abandon himself to inaction and pleasure.

3. A man who is timid and unwilling to suffer, believeth it impossible or useless to fulfil his good resolutions ;

4. Mastered by inordinate self-love, he seeth lions in every path.

5. How many grow weak through shameful cowardice, and tarnish the honour of the most glorious apostolate !

6. And how many, alas, pass their lives

consuming their years and their strength in barren lamentations!

7. All past ages appear to them better than the present, while this is the best and most acceptable time wherein to labour and to suffer for My glory.

8. In every age I have had heroes; and the more they have suffered, the more heroically they bore themselves.

9. Alas, the wicked suffer for the sake of injustice; and wilt thou not suffer for justice' sake?

10. The wicked suffer and strive to do all the injury possible; and hast thou not the courage to suffer for the good of thy brethren?

11. Oh, if thou consider well how the ministers of vice and the emissaries of falsehood exert themselves, I believe thou wouldst set to work in a different way.

12. Be ashamed, if thou hast not yet suffered for the Church that which any one of her wretched enemies have suffered in warring against her.

13. Be ashamed and confounded to see what thou appearest in My presence and in that of the world, more cowardly at times than those who desert virtue from cowardice.

14. Go forth, ye daughters of Sion, and

ye shall see a strange sight—a Christian nourished on My Body, who hath less courage for good than have the defenders and promoters of evil.

15. Come, ye flowers of martyrs, and contemplate a Christian more cowardly than an unbeliever.

16. Have not thine ears heard the hymn of the Church, which exalteth and acclaimeth the valour of virgins and the prowess of martyrs?

17. Having ears, thou hearest not, and having eyes thou seest not; thy heart is hardened.

18. Nevertheless, to confound the weakness of thy clay, I will place before thee the hearts of children firmer than adamant.

19. Cease to pity thyself for thy sufferings in this life. And if it seem to thee that thou hast already suffered much for My Cause, think how often thou hast sinned before Me.

20. In what way canst thou better repair thy negligence than by labouring and suffering for My glory?

21. The true disciple reckoneth not so much what he suffereth, as for what Cause and for Whom he suffereth.

22. How wilt thou know that thy love for Me is true, and how wilt thou enjoy true

liberty, unless thou labour for the raising up of My people and suffer for the honour of My Name?

23. Where My Spirit doth not guide, progress is the road to death.

24. He who liveth not in My grace will find unhappiness in his short-lived happiness.

25. In My Name alone is eternal salvation and assurance of temporal honour.

26. Happy wilt thou be if thou resolve to carry everywhere this holy Name; thou wilt be the glory of thy people and the benefactor of thy country.

27. Oh, how much couldst thou do for My Cause if thou wert ready to suffer and die.

28. He who loveth will lament rather that he hath so little to suffer, than that the vexations of the work are so many.

29. And if thy spirit be weak, set thine eyes on My grace, which is all-powerful.

30. Set thine eyes on My life of suffering and martyrdom, and the greatest sacrifices will appear to thee bearable.

31. And is it not reasonable that thou shouldst suffer for My Name, since I suffered so much for thy temporal good and thine eternal salvation?

32. Renounce sin, and thou wilt not fear death.

33. Renounce sensual pleasures, and thou wilt not fear pain.

34. Renounce a life of vanity, and thou wilt no longer fear labour.

35. If thou seek the truth, fix this ever before thine eyes: work and suffer for thyself and for others.

36. To aim at doing what is profitable, or to begin some glorious enterprise, without having great desire of suffering adversity, is vanity and illusion, not a true resolution of serving Me in the world.

37. Assuredly, that which concerneth My service and the honour of My Church, needeth promptitude and courage; and it is a great sign of virtue not to fear nor to grow faint at meeting difficult obstacles.

38. Show thyself a man with the strength of a Christian, and thou wilt obtain all sweetness from the jaws of the lion.

39. It is by the way of the Cross that men go to Heaven, but it hath become very easy by the sweetness of My counsels.

CHAPTER XX.

OF A PRACTICAL SELF-EXAMINATION, WHICH MY MASTER SETTETH ME.

1. My son, give Me an account of thy life, for I will judge thee at this very hour.

2. Tell Me how thou workest, and reckon with thyself, setting thyself and answering these questions :

3. Do I do much for Christ, for His Church, and for men ?

4. Are all my actions and undertakings always inspired and animated by the spirit of Christ ?

5. Have I sought to learn my duties and my rights, so that I may know what I have to do, and what I can do for the Church and my country ?

6. Do I always take as a practical guidance the latest decrees of the Pope ?

7. Do I avail myself of the services and favours I render, in order to enter into the souls of others, and to lead them to the Lord ?

8. Do I build up illusions for myself, or, on the other hand, do I allow myself to be overcome by idleness and despair ?

9. In my schemes and projects, am I a practical man, an enemy to illusory conquests in the future and to fantastic enterprises?

10. Is the object of my work virtue and profit, or vain honour and self-love?

11. Do I set about drawing the best possible results from the state of affairs and conditions of the present times?

12. Do I help myself and profit by those means which are lawful and permitted to good citizens?

13. Do I obtain all the results possible from opportunities of concerted action, expansion, organization and propaganda?

14. Do I strive to encourage the weak, the inert, the desponding, so that they may devote themselves with constancy to the good work?

15. Give Me an account, My son, I will judge thee according to thy works and intentions.

16. Do I labour to know my work, and to do well what I have to do?

17. Do I let myself be swayed by impressions and by discouragement, when things do not succeed in proportion to the toil and labour?

18. Do men's praises weaken me, or does success delay my career?

19. Do I imprudently desist from my work and efforts, either through repugnance or opposition, or from simple fear of a disturbance?

20. Do I know how to draw great profit from my temptations and trials, and from my mistakes in theory and practice?

21. Do I study the lives and works of the masters of practical life in order to form and animate myself?

22. Do I study the tactics and tendencies of the wicked, so that I may not be surprised into error, and may profit by good organization and more useful methods of procedure?

23. From wishing to be prudent, am I slothful or inefficient; or, from wishing to be active and enterprising, am I imprudent or aggressive?

24. Give Me an account, My son, of what thou dost and of what thou neglectest, for I will judge thee according to thine imperfections and thine omissions.

25. Am I very popular and esteemed, especially by the poor and working-classes?

26. Am I most conciliatory, so as to open a way for myself and to attract recruits?

27. Can I excite and quicken public sympathy, and firmly master my natural aversions?

28. Do I divide the labour in an orderly manner, and make use of co-operation from those who can help me?

29. Do I take the greatest pains over details, which may serve to smooth away difficulties and to give more efficacy to my actions?

30. Are my efforts reasonable and persevering in avoiding or overcoming obstacles?

31. Am I a friend of display and parade, and do I allow myself to be mastered by rivalries, discourtesies and personalities?

32. Do I strive to reduce controversies and disputes to the smallest dimensions and to the purely practical?

33. Do I prudently examine the difficulties of the work and the conditions of the case, so that I may labour with success?

34. Do I know how to forecast the most probable chances, so as not to exhaust myself in vain?

35. Proceed further, My son, if thou wouldst become useful and amend thyself.

36. Do I dwell on points of agreement amongst the good, so that all may work in concert and remove difficulties?

37. Am I an active member of an organization, whose efforts are practical, combined, simultaneous, methodical, persevering, co-

ordinated and directed to the most urgent, necessary and decisive ends?

38. What opposition and difference of opinion may prevail, and break, or render inefficient, the union wherewith Jesus Christ hath united His members?

39. What temporal and earthly interests can separate me from the charity of Christ and from the service of His Church?

40. Do I in practice esteem myself the last of God's servants, needing most to be guided by the Church, and to labour for God and man?

41. Useless and unprofitable servant that I am!

CHAPTER XXI.

THAT I MUST BE VERY HUMBLE TO GIVE DUE GLORY TO CHRIST.

1. Thou must live in great holiness, and thy humility must be very true, if thou desire to sing in thy heart the psalm of Life and of Truth.

2. Ye humble, let us glorify God,
   The God of the humble,
   And our works shall be true—
   The works of our wisdom.

3. Ye humble, let us glorify God,
   The God of the humble,
   And our works shall be just and holy—
   The works of our justice.

4. Ye humble, let us glorify God,
   The God of the humble,
   And our works shall be prudent—
   The works of our prudence.

5. Ye humble, let us glorify God,
   The God of the humble,
   And our works shall be strong—
   The works of our fortitude.

6. Ye humble, let us glorify God,
   The God of the humble,
   And our works shall be profitable—
   The works of our perseverance.

7. Ye humble, let us glorify God,
   The God of the humble,
   And our works shall be lasting—
   The works of our hope.

8. Ye humble, let us glorify God,
   The God of the humble,
   And our works shall be fruitful—
   The works of our apostolate.

9. Ye humble, let us glorify God,
   The God of the humble,
   And our works shall be rewarded—
   The works of our love to men.

10. Ye humble, let us glorify God,
    The God of the humble,
    As He is glorified in His glory,
    For ever and ever.   Amen.

BOOK THE THIRD.

Inquire Pacem—" Seek after Peace."

Psalm xxxiii. 15.

CHAPTER I.

OF SOME CONSIDERATIONS TO EXPAND THE WINGS OF TRUE ZEAL.

1. Seek to do good, and thou wilt at the same time imitate Me.

2. If thou be light, enlighten; if thou be fire, melt; if thou be water, refresh; if thou be salt, cleanse and preserve the purity of souls.

3. Examine thy talents, and study the greatest needs.

4. The deeper thou goest, the more wilt thou find that merely social and human remedies only serve to avoid a few ills.

5. The best way of solving social problems is to make men better from within.

6. Social action will be as much more social, efficacious and profitable, as it containeth human gain and supernatural influence.

7. I say to thee, if thou art a great painter and always a good Catholic, thou wilt have more profit than an orator by his discourse.

8. I say to thee, if thou art a great scholar and a good Catholic, thou wilt serve

My cause better than he who showeth himself very zealous in words.

9. I say to thee, if thou art a great legislator and show thyself a good Catholic, thou wilt obtain more results than he who only showeth himself very devout.

10. Neglect Me not in the great universities; neglect Me not in the great problems of the day; neglect Me not in great assemblies; neglect Me not in the great interests of life.

11. If science demand learning, and finance demand application, and study demand problems, and action demand efforts; I also must demand what is Mine, and I neither permit anything to be kept back from Me, nor allow My servants to neglect Me.

12. Where shouldst thou glorify Me? Where shouldst thou make thine influence felt? Where should ye make it known that ye are sons of Power, of Knowledge, of Goodness, and of the Cause of eternal Peace? Everywhere.

13. Some imagine that they need only honour Me in their acts of piety: and that with all the rest they need not serve the cause of peace among men, and between men and God; and their illusion is a deceit.

14. Perform but one good public act, and thou wilt find that others will make ten good interior acts.

15. Infuse Catholicism into science, into politics, into industry, into all branches of human activity, and thou wilt do a great act of charity.

16. Science, arts, commerce, all human activities are demanding great alms of uprightness, personal goodness and sanctity: and who is able to give them but thou?

17. I, the Word of the Father, equal to the Father, and eternal Son of God, made Myself man, and in My Person both remain united, man and God, earth and Heaven; and art thou willing to abandon for ever, and leave in possession of the wicked, all social activity, which originally came from the Eternal Energy, the Infinite Life, the Divine Assistance, the Essential Light.

CHAPTER II.

OF THE RICHES CONTAINED IN THE TREASURE OF TRUE PEACE.

1. My peace, dear son, is a treasure hidden from the eyes of turbulent men and lovers of self.

2. It declareth and discovereth itself to the lowly and simple of heart.

3. If thou desire that My peace reign in thy spirit, master thy passions and rule thy life according to My precepts.

4. If thou desire that My peace be in thy work, labour with method and for the sake of men.

5. If thou desire that it reign in thy friends, give a good example and sacrifice thine own pleasures.

6. My peace is the reward of the good, and the recompense for the virtues of the nation.

7. My peace germinateth in the warmth of active self-sacrifice.

8. It is nourished by the conquest over self and over disorder.

9. It is defended by a working faith; it resteth in transforming charity.

10. Noiselessly doth it enter into hearts, and it conquereth its enemy for his good.

11. It maketh the soul fruitful and the body strong.

12. It exalteth the humble, and filleth with good things the poor of spirit.

13. It tempereth the power of rulers, and dilateth the hearts of subjects.

14. It uniteth men in good, and giveth life and soul to laws.

15. It despiseth what is worthless, and uplifteth to the eternal and divine.

16. My peace, finally, leadeth men to God, and giveth them possession of God Himself.

CHAPTER III.

OF SOME THINGS WHICH MY MASTER TELLETH ME, THAT I MAY WORK FOR PEACE.

1. Son, I am the first to whom liberty should be assured; I am the first to whom reverence should be given; I am the first whose influence should be efficacious.

2. The more My liberty is recognised, the more shall the nations be free; the more

My rights are respected, the more shall
human rights be respected; the more My
influence is felt, the more shall the influence
of each one be profitable and efficacious.

3. Love duty, and thou shalt find thy
rights; seek obedience, and thou shalt find
order; vindicate silence, and thou shalt find
activity; maintain justice for all classes, and
thou shalt find peace.

4. Labour zealously; guide and establish
mutual unity in My doctrine and My virtues,
and thou shalt obtain an everlasting reward.

5. Son, if thou bear thyself as My faithful
friend, glory for glory, honour for honour,
profit for service shalt thou obtain.

6. The more thou glorify Me with extrinsic
glory, and the more thou serve Me in profit-
ing thy neighbour, the more will I give
thee intrinsic glory and most profitable
virtue.

7. Two things are marvels beyond concep-
tion to Mine angels: that I have so loved
you, and that man is so narrow of heart and
of so little understanding.

8. Be prudent, be wise, and attend to
affairs while yet thou hast time.

9. If thou art not very diligent, how canst
thou know the meaning of rest? If thou
art not very useful, how canst thou be My

disciple? If thou labour not for My Cause, how shalt thou merit victory?

10. Thou shalt rest in My peace, if thou make thyself an apostle of salvation and peace.

11. My peace is not as the world promiseth, but as victory over the world giveth.

12. The more evil is free, the less will good be free.

13. The less good is free, the less will liberty be free.

14. The less liberty is free, the less will justice be free.

15. The less justice is free, the less will duty be free.

16. The less duty is free, the less will good, and the fruitfulness of peace and true liberty hold sway.

CHAPTER IV.

OF WHAT I SHALL BE ABLE TO PRACTISE, IF I UNDERSTAND.

1. What concerneth the influence of My Kingdom in this world, is like unto that which befalleth a fisherman who goeth a-fishing.

2. The fisherman will not wait for the fish to come to his house.

3. But he taketh his nets and goeth where he knoweth the fish to be.

4. There will he set the best bait and therefore trust in hope.

5. He beginneth by arming himself with patience, and doth not cry out nor make a disturbance.

6. If God bless his labour, he temperately rejoiceth thereat.

7. If he take nothing, he returneth another time with more joy and eagerness.

8. The kingdom of Christian effort is like unto a good fisherman who desireth to do well when he desireth to fish.

9. What concerneth the influence of My Kingdom in this world, is like unto a good shepherd.

10. The shepherd is very peaceful and taketh delight in the flock that he desireth to pasture.

11. He aimeth not at overburdening any-one nor at injuring his sheep.

12. Rather will he gently lead them to where there is good pasture.

13. If one of his sheep go astray, he seeketh it; if one be sick, he helpeth it as far as he can.

14. He watcheth without agitation and seeketh ever the good of his flock.

15. If they come to a bad path, he guideth them; if there be danger, he defendeth them.

16. And he will even give his life for the good of his sheep.

17. The kingdom of Christian effort in this world is like unto a shepherd, who is careful to imitate Me in his actions.

CHAPTER V.

OF WHAT LOVE IS, AND HOW FAR IT CAN EXTEND.

1. Love waiteth not for chances of doing good, but seeketh them; it doth not fear them, but welcometh them; it doth not flee them, but profiteth by them.

2. Love without deeds is either no love, or it suffereth and consumeth itself.

3. Love needeth no spur nor reward; to love is its life and its repose.

4. Generosity without love is deceit or vanity,—a love without loving,—how doth it know that it is love?

5. Study, then, My son, to love much. Because I loved, I gave Myself for men, and I laboured and suffered for all.

6. Nevertheless, My mission especially concerneth men. I called the shepherds and the kings, I chose and united the Apostles, I devoted Myself by preference to forming a mystical and social body amongst men.

7. Son, if thou love Me, labour for men. Son, if thou love Me, labour much amongst men. Son, if thou love Me more than others, labour also to obtain the eternal salvation of women.

8. If thou love Me exceedingly, study how women can do good to men.

CHAPTER VI.

BY WHAT WAY I CAN GO TO MEET PEACE.

1. Give ear to Me, I will speak to thee words of peace, for I am the Word of the living God.

2. Peace in this life resteth on two pillars, law and duty.

3. Peace is guarded by two sentinels, love

in him who commandeth and humility in him who obeyeth.

4. Peace is held up by two forces, justice in the mighty and loyalty in the lowly.

5. Peace is maintained as between brothers, by the generous virtue of the wealthy and the learned, and by the patience and the gratitude of the poor and the unlearned.

6. But, My son, thou must observe that where there is neither faith nor charity, there is no life of grace.

7. And where there is no life of grace, there is no true virtue.

8. And where there is no true virtue, there is no true freedom.

9. And where there is no true freedom, there is no respect for law.

10. And where there is no respect for law, there no man can fulfil his duty.

11. And where men cannot fulfil their duty, there is no order.

12. And where there is no order, there is no unity in the commonwealth.

13. And where there is no true unity, there is no harmony.

14. And where there is no harmony, there is no peace, but despair and confusion, and fury, and contradiction, and vengeance, and

suffering without consolation or profit, a sharing beforehand in the evils of Hell.

15. If thou understand this, thou wilt be able to do much for Peace.

CHAPTER VII.

OF SOME COUNSELS WHICH I MUST OFTEN USE.

1. Son, in the combined action of the Church, if thou be not doing, thou art hindering and undoing.

2. If thou exert not thyself to act, but at most confine thyself to weeping or criticising, they will tell thee that the principles thou professest are not good, or that thou livest not according to the virtue they possess.

3. Goodness ever tendeth to well-doing; it is ever active, it must be working either within or without.

4. But there are some who, instead of being men of action, are causes of agitation.

5. They think they work much, when they disturb many.

6. To be of use to My Cause, thou must avoid four things above all: indecision, inaction, inconstancy, and dissensions amongst those who might help thee.

7. Thou wilt avoid such grave faults by knowing how to reflect, by knowing how to love, by knowing how to labour, by knowing how to suffer.

8. Never deem thyself so just, that thou sin by excess; nor so necessary, that thou fail by defect.

9. Thou must not repulse those, whom I do not repulse.

10. Thou must not condemn those, to whom I refuse not My grace.

11. Thou must not repel those, whom I strive to attract.

12. Bring to pass that he who giveth thee as two, may labour as four,[1] and each time with more purity of intention.

13. Son, if thou hast to learn from unbelievers, thou wilt cut a sorry figure, and wilt always be late in using means and applying remedies.

---

[1] Translator's note.—In his meditation on the "Three Classes of Men," St. Ignatius speaks of "couples" of men.

CHAPTER VIII.

HOW I MUST BLESS THE LORD IN ALL THINGS.

1. Son, if thou art alone, rejoice in thy God, and in spirit; but if thou art with thy brethren, neglect not to sing the praises due to Me.

2. Bless Jesus Christ, Oh ye Bishops:
    Bless Him, ye Bishops and dioceses.

3. Bless Jesus Christ, Oh ye parish clergy:
    Bless Him, ye parish clergy and people.

4. Bless Jesus Christ, Oh ye priests:
    Bless Him, ye priests and lay-folk.

5. Bless Jesus Christ, Oh ye religious:
    Bless Him, ye religious and confra-
    ternities.

6. Bless Jesus Christ, Oh ye of the contem-
    plative life:
    Bless Him with your penances.

7. Bless Jesus Christ, Oh ye of the active
    life:
    Bless Him with your undertakings.

8. Bless Jesus Christ, Oh ye strong:
    Bless Him with your combats.

9. Bless Jesus Christ, Oh ye learned:
    Bless Him with your writings.

10. Bless Jesus Christ, Oh ye artists:
Bless Him with your works.

11. Bless Jesus Christ, Oh ye fathers:
Bless Him with your families.

12. Bless Jesus Christ, Oh ye masters:
Bless Him with your pupils.

13. Bless Jesus Christ, Oh ye first-born:
Bless Him with your brothers.

14. Bless Jesus Christ, Oh ye rich:
Bless Him with your alms.

15. Bless Jesus Christ, Oh ye poor:
Bless Him with your toil.

16. Bless Jesus Christ, Oh ye mighty:
Bless Him with your example.

17. Bless Jesus Christ, Oh ye rulers:
Bless Him with your subjects.

18. Let us bless Jesus Christ in private and
in public:
Let us bless Him in life and in death.

19. Let us bless Him in our words and
works:
And through all eternity.   Amen.

CHAPTER IX.

HOW I MUST PROCEED WITH CAUTION TO
BECOME HUMBLE AND SERVICEABLE.

1. If thou desire not to act frivolously nor to compromise thyself, strive to know the world very thoroughly; so that, without harm to thy conscience, thou mayest work happily for My Cause.

2. Nothing so well showeth what a man is worth as contempt or praise.

3. Nothing so well showeth what he desireth, as riches or misfortune.

4. Nothing so well showeth what he thinketh, as slander or applause.

5. Nothing so well showeth his friendship, as forgetfulness or self-denial.

6. Nothing so well showeth his fervour, as silence or clamour.

7. Nothing so well showeth his intentions, as sudden attack or calumny.

8. Proceed not lightly in judging others, nor set thyself to pry into their lives.

9. If thou desire more help from others, or to fit them for My Cause, thou must not approach them without tact.

10. The upright man thinketh clearly and

uprightly, and yieldeth not himself body and soul to others.

11. When thou intendest to do good to any one, take heed first that thine own pulse be normal, and then thou canst see whether the other have fever.

12. The more thou despise thyself, the more defects shalt thou find in thyself.

13. The more thou know thyself, the less wilt thou despise others for their faults.

14. The more thou be convinced of the malice of this world, the more wilt thou arm thyself with prayer and self-examination.

15. If in swimming thou try to draw another from the flood, watch well that thou be not thyself drowned.

CHAPTER X.

THAT I MUST GUARD MYSELF AGAINST ILLUSION IN GOOD WORKS.

1. Son, be not deceived by appearances nor by thy personal inclinations.

2. Services of simple usefulness are often better and more pleasing in Mine eyes, than those of mere showy piety.

3. In all thy works first carefully examine what thou hast first to do.

4. Thou must undertake in preference that which will produce the most certain and true results.

5. Many things are undertaken more from vanity than from a spirit of solid piety.

6. How shall a cathedral serve thee for My glory, if the poor have not a parish church?

7. Sometimes, it is true, it is fitting to erect an immense basilica, but at others a poor chapel.

8. Those judge rightly in these things, whose eyes are clear.

9. Watch well that thou labour in an especial manner at those things which make thy neighbour secure.

10. Watch well that thou labour to impede the wicked, who have power to destroy what is fundamental.

11. If thou build much, and the wicked are left at liberty, both thy church and Mine will be swept away together.

12. What is held to be the highest good by the perverse? Their only concern is for their belly.

13. Their belly is the God of their crimes

and robberies; their belly is the aim of their deceits and empty promises.

14. But, alas, thou hast not been able to learn from the serpent, and thou deemest still that folly is goodness.

CHAPTER XI.

IN HOW MANY WAYS I CAN CO-OPERATE IN THE GENERAL CATHOLIC MOVEMENT.

1. If thou have no influence over the people, how will they follow thee with constancy?

2. If thou canst not draw the masses, how will they desire to enrol themselves freely in thine army?

3. It is not enough that thy Cause be good: thou thyself must inspire confidence.

4. The will of its own nature tendeth thither, where talent and power are found.

5. Thou wilt not lack followers, if thou watch over the interests of all.

6. To labour for good organization is to multiply forces.

7. To labour in unison with many is to increase a hundred-fold the powers of each.

8. He who holdeth civil authority, will do good or do evil a thousand-fold.

9. Without numbers there can be no army: without a great army, no safety for mankind.

10. Three men loyal to one, avail more than three thousand who will submit to no yoke.

11. Son, union must tend to give expansion and efficacy to a movement, not to impede and paralyse it.

12. If thou aim at too perfect conformity, there may perchance be no moving hand or foot.

13. What is done with much pleasure, is carried on with more constancy and fruit.

14. All have not the same power, but practice increaseth ability.

15. He who cannot give his vote, can lead others to vote;

16. He who cannot speak in public, can applaud;

17. He who cannot command, can augment the ranks.

18. If thou canst distinguish between the useful and the useless, thou wilt obtain much profit.

19. He who examineth himself, shall find; he who prepareth himself, shall not lose his

time; he who measureth the distance, shall
not walk at a venture.

20. Great men have served Me in all ages:
do thou study their works.

CHAPTER XII.

SOME COUNSELS WHICH WILL SERVE ME IN THE STRUGGLE FOR PEACE.

1. Son, where My rights triumph not,
no duty will be respected.

2. Where duties which I have imposed
are not fulfilled, thou wilt not be able to
obtain thy rights.

3. Where I am not free, thou wilt be a
slave of evil.

4. Where impiety beginneth to conquer,
it will end by persecuting thee.

5. Neutrality is impossible; it is a contradiction in terms.

6. No one opposeth My rights more
insidiously than he who pleadeth for
neutrality.

7. He who claimeth to be neutral in
religious questions, tendeth at one blow to

destroy all the influence of My mission and My redemption.

8. The height of all contempt and injustice is the wickedness which would clothe itself in an ill-concealed indifference.

9. All will esteem liberty an evil, where freedom for doing good reigneth not.

10. Combat the abundance of ills by good works.

11. Combat the indifference of a bad conscience by an abundance of good works.

12. Do not believe in truces: to suspend the struggle is to surrender one's arms and yield to the enemy.

13. If thou be not skilled in fighting, do good works on all sides.

14. But if thou canst fight, then stoutly defend My rights, and thou wilt be assured of thine own.

15. Son, if My Church be not free, thou thyself wilt never enjoy liberty.

16. If My Church cannot exercise her rights, thou wilt never succeed in making thy conscience respected.

17. If thou learn not to strive for the good, then wilt thou fall into the slavery of evil.

18. The liberty of truth setteth free those who can acquire that same true liberty.

19. Reflect much in a little time; labour much with gentleness; abide always in My presence; and act always with constancy.

20. If thou desire one thing to-day and another to-morrow, thou wilt desire much and achieve little.

21. If thou desire to excel in many directions, thou wilt speak without measure and convince no one.

22. Examine thy dispositions: I chose fishermen, and I sent them to fish for men.

CHAPTER XIII.

OF THE TACTICS I MUST EMPLOY FOR THE GOOD OF THE WHOLE WORLD.

1. I have already told thee many things; but thou art still a novice.

2. Since numbers are strength, find lawful means to gain help from many.

3. The wicked will readily leave thee with mere goodness of principle, if thou leave them a free field for their excesses.

4. As soon as the wicked acquire power, they will mock at thy rights.

5. If thou canst guard the good by means

of many, work in unison with all and thou wilt do good to many.

6. When a good springeth from a common effort, the gain is the more welcome.

7. What a man acquireth by his own labour, he holdeth in more esteem.

8. Nothing more disposeth a man to action than the defence of his own rights.

9. He who desireth not to be the slave of evil, must labour and struggle for the good.

10. To look for liberty and tolerance from the unbeliever, is to expect good fruit from a bad tree.

11. When evil conquereth, liberty perisheth.

12. Nor can there be tolerance where wickedness raiseth its head with arrogance.

13. Where circumstances offer thee thy lawful rights, exercise thy duties.

14. What will become of the little ones? What will become of the weak? What will become of the poor, if wickedness mocketh the good?

15. It is often better to do what is most urgent and necessary, not what is most excellent.

16. If the masses work for the popular welfare, when they are working for the Church, they will feel more encouraged, and their work will be ennobled.

17. If thou stand still awaiting the realization of thine ideal, thou wilt be crushed by the weight of brute force.

18. If thou always persist in being wedded to form, thou wilt ever remain without substance.

19. One thing is possible to-day: thy progress will make another possible to-morrow.

20. He who holdeth the roots, holdeth the tree; he who holdeth individuals, holdeth the masses.

21. He who worketh amongst the masses for My Cause will save society, and with it all classes of men.

22. Tell Me, My son, since victory in many matters dependeth on one vote, why dost thou not seek a hundred?

23. If thou desire to attack all Mine enemies at once, thou wilt conquer none of them.

24. The first thou must attack is the one thou canst most easily conquer.

25. Do now what befitteth the moment; another time will come after.

26. If thou desire to hinder all evils, thou wilt obstruct thyself and remain paralyzed.

27. When two of you fight the same enemy, help one another.

28. The best method of fighting thine opponent is to strive to do him good and to bring him back to the right path.

29. If the vanquished can rejoice in thy victory, thou hast obtained two glorious triumphs.

30. Blessed is he whose heart is on fire with charity; his sword shall be love and truth.

CHAPTER XIV.

WHAT I CAN DO BY MYSELF AND WITH OTHERS.

1. My son, a united effort badly prepared in most cases only serveth to make the victory of the wicked more noisy and effectual.

2. Regular and secure effects are only obtained when each soldier knoweth and seeketh to exercise his own duty in the strife.

3. When unity is more observed, then will individuals and the whole people be more easily established in good.

4. Lack of instruction, idleness, cowardice

and the interests of the moment, are the worst enemies to general action and to steady progress in good.

5. The secret of victory lieth not in the coming of a great man, nor in imagining that he should surprise thee with his prowess.

6. I Myself appeared as the most wondrous of all prodigies; I Myself was awaited from the beginning of the world; yet those who expected Me failed to recognise Me.

7. Weak souls and sluggards ever desire miracles, and lovers of self always talk of things to come.

8. The remedy lieth not in vain hopes, nor in trusting to others, but in thine own labours, strengthened by union and blessed and confirmed by My grace.

9. The most useful and almost always needful, is the individual apostolate, so as to found a numerous, very simple and very practical association.

10. Few are capable of organizing, inspiring, and uniting many in active work; but all can take part in the practical training of first one and then another in religious and civil duties.

11. If a man bewail the lack of good combinations, let him take good heed that he cause no divisions in those which already

exist, nor interfere by opposing the formation of the most suitable.

12. Did each one undeceive, enlighten,
strengthen and convert to good but one
other, no one would think of factions, and
all society would be filled with associations.

13. Did each one bring one other to
practise religious virtues and social duties,
none would complain that they lacked
strength to follow the right path.

14. Did each family give a good example
in the field of virtue, many evils would be
avoided.

15. I called Mine Apostles one by one,
and I told each privately and at the right
moment what was most fitting for him.

16. Pray most frequently in common, sing
often in unison, and let each one labour as
if all the good hoped for depended on him
alone.

17. If there be too many social bodies,
there will be little general movement, want
of unity and great confusion in the same
individuals.

18. Great works are carried out by
few : general undertakings are carried out
by all uniting.

19. In every conversation, on every
journey, in every business, in every social

visit, something can be done towards the gaining and training of individuals, towards the formation of religious practices, the proper use of rights, and the easy and exact fulfilment of social duties.

20. Ponder My life, and thou wilt find an abundance of examples which confirm My teaching.

CHAPTER XV.

HOW I MUST ENTER UPON AND INCREASE MY WORK TO RESTORE ALL.

1. My son, I am about to tell thee many truths in very few and simple words: when thou readest them, take heed to meditate on them, and neglect not to put them into practice.

2. Where thou canst not succeed in establishing My Name, strive to bring in My Church.

3. Where thou canst not succeed in establishing My Church, strive to bring in My teaching.

4. Where thou canst not succeed in establishing My teaching, strive to bring in My virtues.

5. Where thou canst not succeed in establishing My virtues, strive to bring in My great sacrifices.

6. Where thou canst not succeed in establishing My great sacrifices, strive to bring in My love of the sick and the poor.

7. Where thou canst not succeed in establishing My love of the sick and the poor, strive to bring in My sweet words.

8. Where thou canst not succeed in establishing My sweet words, strive to bring in the charm and simplicity of My Person.

9. Where thou canst not succeed in establishing the charm and simplicity of My Person, strive to bring in thy good works.

10. Where thou canst not succeed in establishing thy good works, strive to bring in thine influence.

11. Where thou canst not succeed in establishing thine influence, strive to bring in thy good arguments.

12. Where thou canst not succeed in establishing thy good arguments, strive to bring in thy kindly tact.

13. Where thou canst not succeed in establishing thy kindly tact, strive to bring in thy good example.

14. Where thou canst not succeed in

establishing thy good example, strive to bring in thy most faithful friends.

15. Where thou canst not succeed in establishing thy most faithful friends, strive to bring in true science.

16. Where thou canst not succeed in establishing true science, strive to bring in order in the utility of interests.

17. Where thou canst not succeed in establishing order in the utility of interests, strive to bring in moderation in amusements.

18. Where thou canst not succeed in establishing moderation in amusements, strive to diminish the number of sins.

19. Do at all times and in all places, all the good that thou canst do; hinder at all times and in all places, all the evil thou canst hinder; serve My Cause at all times and in all places, by all means whereby thou canst serve it. Despise no means, whether good or indifferent, if, without injury to thy conscience and without scandal to thy neighbour, thou canst employ them for conquering.

20. "Whether ye eat or drink, or whatsoever else ye do," pray always in spirit, and glorify Me by the sincerity of thine intention and thine actions, so that thou

mayest rejoice in thy God in this life and eternally.

21. It profiteth much frequently to say: "What can I do for Christ in this position? What can I do for Christ in this matter? What can I do for Christ with these means and in these circumstances? What can I do, lastly, for Christ, in the presence of these persons, with them, in them and for them, and for the glory and profit of the cause of Christ?

22. "What would the great Paul have done here? What would the great Francis Xavier have suffered now? What would the great Francis of Sales have said, and how would he have said it?" Thou must learn from My friends. The glory of their souls, filled with My spirit, overflowed in their actions.

23. Thou wilt learn more by loving than by much reading and study;

24. But it serveth much to read and study in the book of My life, to know how to love Me.

25. Then wilt thou avoid many and useless disputes, and wilt devote thyself to fruitful sacrifices and profitable actions.

26. Oh, what folly to think thou canst triumph over malice and error without

possessing much divine science, and much practice in handling the human weapons of the most divine love.

27. If thou wouldst do aught, thou must often begin with the indifferent, so as to proceed to the good: continue with the good, so as to proceed to the better: and strive to establish the best firmly and from within, so as not to fall back into the imperfect, into the indifferent and even into the worst.

28. If without preparation thou aim at all, thou wilt obtain nothing. In seeking always the perfect in every case, thou wouldst have often to combat not only evil, but likewise good; and this would leave thee without the good and also without the best.

29. The supernatural elevateth, purifieth and perfecteth human good, and human good is ennobled and made more useful when it serveth the supernatural.

CHAPTER XVI.

OF SOME SIMILITUDES FOR BECOMING A MAN OF GOOD WORKS.

1. The kingdom of Christian activity is like unto a good swimmer, who diveth to the bottom of the water to save a drowning man, and striveth with his precious burden to reach the seashore.

2. The kingdom of Christian activity is like unto a light, which consumeth itself to send its influence in all directions, without receiving any injury from the darkness or from the filth of sewers.

3. The kingdom of Christian activity is like unto a whirlwind which is ever in movement, and which constantly increaseth in force as it advanceth in the best direction.

4. The man who can meditate showeth what he hath learned by the perfection with which he afterwards setteth to work.

CHAPTER XVII.

THAT I MUST ATTEND TO WHAT IS BELOW IN ORDER TO ATTAIN TO WHAT IS ON HIGH.

1. He who desireth to be profitable and useful must follow My steps, imitating My example and My lessons.

2. Maintain lofty ideals in such a manner as not to contemn the smallest details.

3. Defend higher interests in such a manner as not to neglect the lower. And I will even say to thee, if thou wouldst well defend the former, begin by watching over the latter.

4. He who goeth about with excessive anxiety seeking his daily food, findeth it difficult to attend to his soul.

5. How will the poor man believe thou desirest his eternal salvation, if thou help him not to obtain what he needeth on earth?

6. If the unbeliever exert himself more than thou for the great material interests, thou wilt with difficulty gain credit in moral good.

7. Not by spiritual good alone doth man live, but necessarily also by bodily means.

8. The higher order destroyeth not the lower, but giveth it dignity and greater force.

9. Truly, what concerneth moral perfection must be regarded as the supreme good of a reasonable creature.

10. If the soul give life to the body, the body likewise helpeth the soul in this life.

11. The crowd followed Me desiring to hear My teachings, but I had compassion on their bodily needs.

12. It is certain that where great virtues flourish, good corn will be but little wanting.

CHAPTER XVIII.

OF THE MEANS I HAVE TO USE TO BE A GOOD MAN OF GOOD WORKS.

1. My son, I preached in words, yet did I not cease to teach and to draw men by My virtues and example.

2. If thou know to-day of any lawful means, perhaps most useful and timely for human affairs, leave it not in the power of the enemy, whether this man or that be the

author of the device in the eyes of the world.

3. Hast thou not heard how often the wicked blaspheme Me? Then for the ruin of men, they often imitate Me, and yet falsify the works of My grace and My example.

4. How much then must thou not profit from the most useful resources, imitating Me in a diligent zeal for souls.

5. Thou must not despise any means because they are new, or because they have been used till now by the ungodly; but only if they are unseemly to thy position, or if they gainsay the holiness of My teaching.

6. In very truth, it had been better if thou, moved by zeal for My Cause, hadst been the first to contrive and put in practice these methods of action, if they are of themselves indifferent and yet useful.

7. But since they are already in lawful use, and are so profitable and fruitful, apply them not as mere remedies, but as most efficient instruments.

8. Son, what is only practised and admitted as a mere prescription and medicine, is often applied and employed as a simple condiment, not from a fervent desire of serving Me.

9. If there appear some danger in these means, because their abuse is easy, or from thine habitual disposition to evil, it is well that thou be prepared betimes, and that thou proceed with caution and with an upright heart.

10. But, My son, if it be right to fear, it is also necessary to act.

11. If it be right to guard against danger, it is likewise needful to profit by the good.

12. If it be good and reasonable to preserve the better, it is also very requisite to hinder the worse.

13. If the new always trouble thee, because it is new, how wilt thou sway the multitude with thine influence and activity?

14. My son, I preached in words, and Mine Apostles neglected not to teach by writing.

15. I visited the sick in their own abodes; My disciples visited them and also founded hospitals.

16. I set poverty on a throne higher than the skies, and My disciples have raised buildings for the children of the poor.

17. How mighty is the mind of man, when he maketh himself the master, and not the slave of human means!

18. If in what is left to thy free and well-ordered will, thou always aim at following the same direction, thou wilt some day stumble against obstacles and break thy head.

19. Thou must assuredly persist in what is solid and unchanging, and labour with the temporal for the eternal.

20. Do good with what thou hast, and thou wilt obtain what thou desirest.

21. I shall come and shall not delay: do thou profit by the time.

22. The good servant despiseth not small things.

23. From desire of pleasing Me, what did not My loyal servant Paul do?

24. I kept silence at the tribunals; and My Apostle, though he desired martyrdom, appealed as a Roman citizen to Cæsar in order to serve Me.

25. Too much and uselessly dost thou lament that the ungodly misuse certain means.

26. If thou contemplate the fountains of My grace, the holy Sacraments, thou wilt see what kind of instruments I have chosen.

27. Have not sinners abused the fruits of the earth? And yet what hath not My

boundless love made of them as food for thy soul?

28. Often thou murmurest against the most useful methods, and meanwhile, clever unbelievers pervert many with them, and the people are lost.

29. Oh! how thy self-love deceiveth thee, and the personal inclination which mastereth thee.

30. Hadst thou a great spirit of true self-sacrifice, thou wouldst not conceal under empty excuses, thy lack of love for study and for action.

31. What hast thou gained, when thou hast contemned and anathematized the most suitable methods of thy time and the most influential and effective treatment for working from soul to soul, and for labouring in many directions at once?

32. The cause of My Peace in the world is deserted, while the wicked laugh at thine unreasoning obstinacy and at thy want of foresight and sound judgment.

33. If thou wilt not, or canst not labour with the most profitable and attractive instruments, how dost thou expect to do anything with the most inefficient and blunted?

34. But thou art rashly determined to

venture against Goliath with five pebbles!
If thou canst do so much, begin, like David,
by practising thyself and testing thy strength
against lions.

35. Thou wilt gain the favours of My
special Providence, when thou despiseth
not the resources of My general Providence

36. Arise and walk! Seek, study, form,
diffuse, organise, transform, establish and
attract for the good of My Cause!

37. Seek the most pure, the most prudent,
the most intelligent, the most active and
profitable zeal. Measure its breadth, go
over its length to see how far it extendeth;
penetrate to its greatest depth and rise by
the light of faith to see how high it mounteth.

38. If thou follow the counsels of My
Church, thou wilt never go astray.

39. If thou labour according to the will of
My Vicar on earth, thy efforts will be neither
useless nor harmful.

40. More is obtained by joining in the
Unity of My infallible and universal Church,
than by all that is greatest and most powerful when unruly.

41. The truest, most certain and most
efficient antidote to all excess of private
judgment and all abuse of self-will, lieth in
submitting without reserve, and obeying

without excuse, with full adhesion of mind and sincere affection of heart, the supreme and infallible representative of My divine Person and Authority.

42. Son, thou deemest at times that thou knowest much, and yet thou knowest not as much as My Church knoweth.

43. Remember, My son, that the greatest enemies to thine action are vanity and frivolity, obstinacy of private judgment, imprudent fears, unmeasured anxieties, work done from impulse, and persistence in applying inordinate or useless means.

CHAPTER XIX.

THE PSALM OF BROTHERLY LOVE, WHICH MY MASTER TEACHETH ME.

1. Son, if thou desire to be My disciple, conform thyself to My spirit and teaching.

2. And so that thou mayest the more conform thyself, repeat often with truth on thy lips and acts of thine affection:

3. O Jesus, Who hast said, " By this shall all men know that you are My disciples, if

you have love one for another,"[1] kindle
and keep alive in our breasts the fire of
true charity. Amen.

4. Let us all love one another for Jesus
   And in Jesus, our Love and Salvation;
   For the glory of Christ
   And the prosperity of His Church.
   Amen.

5. Let us ever bear with one another for
   Jesus
   And in Jesus, our Good and Redemp-
   tion;
   For the glory of Christ
   And the prosperity of His Church.
   Amen.

6. Let us all help one another for Jesus
   And in Jesus, our Strength and Reward;
   For the glory of Christ
   And the prosperity of His Church.
   Amen.

7. Let us ever protect one another for
   Jesus
   And in Jesus, our Shield and Pro-
   tection;
   For the glory of Christ
   And the prosperity of His Church.
   Amen.

---

[1] St. John xiii. 35.

8. Let us all console one another for Jesus
And in Jesus, our Bliss and Consolation;
For the glory of Christ
And the prosperity of His Church.
Amen.

9. Let us ever pardon one another for Jesus
And in Jesus, our Peace and Oblation;
For the glory of Christ
And the prosperity of His Church.
Amen.

10. Let us all unite with one another for Jesus
And in Jesus, our Life and eternal Glory;
For the glory of Christ
And the prosperity of His Church.
Amen.

11. Let us ever put into practice, for the social honour of the most Holy Name of Jesus, the sweet teachings of the science of love, which our most loving Jesus hath left us in the words of His Divine Heart, in the example of His works and virtues, and in the sacrifices of His most holy life, devoting Himself for us, His very enemies, even to the death of the Cross. Amen.

12. This wilt thou repeat often, My son, with truth on thy lips and with works in thy hands, if thou desire to conform thyself to My teaching and Spirit.

CHAPTER XX.

HOW I MUST BE ON MY GUARD, IF I DESIRE TO TRIUMPH WITH MY MASTER.

1. Strive, My son, to live not on words, but rather on great realities.

2. Strive to study the under-currents of the age, to know whither thou must direct thine efforts.

3. There are things which always remain, and there are others which pass away, without injury to the eternal.

4. Do not aim at subjecting the supernatural and eternal to the accidental and passing.

5. If thou know how to prepare thyself, thou wilt be freed from many surprises.

6. If thou study the future, thou wilt advance quickly in many things.

7. Certain things are evil in themselves, and to these thou must never conform ;

8. Others, indifferent and even very useful, are perverted through the disorder of men.

9. Those which are only evil by the wickedness of the ungodly, thou canst by My grace convert to good;

10. If thou do not make them good and hold them in thy hands, they will harm thee greatly, for the malice of the wicked is very crafty.

11. The ungodly preferreth to injure thee with that which is of general utility, rather than with that which is evil in itself.

12. When he seeth himself in possession of victory, then will he put thee to confusion, if he can, with all the fury of the most wicked malice.

13. Thou wilt know much if thou know how to obey My Vicar; to him have I promised My special assistance.

14. When thou art in doubt whether thou shalt succeed or no, go to the Seer, to him who seeth from the highest point of vantage, for he is My Vicar; and suffer not thyself to be deceived by empty speeches nor by the rash judgments of men.

15. If it seem to thee that thine enemies are very powerful and wicked, have great fervour, great purity of intention, and be alert and cautious.

16. The enemy can only conquer thee, when he succeedeth in making thee inordinate, weak or hopeless, or when he induceth thee to follow him in using some unworthy means.

17. When thou conquerest thyself, I conquer the wicked. When the wicked seem to conquer, if thou do thy duty, I conquer them even in thee thyself.

18. The final victory, whether men will it or no, is always Mine.

19. Labour then, labour much and ever more; watch for My Cause, and thou watchest for thyself.

CHAPTER XXI.

OF THE LESSONS GIVEN ME BY THE CHARITY OF CHRIST.

1. Oh Charity which art come down from Heaven for the love of men, teach their hearts to love!

2. The more humble the beginnings, and the more unselfish the aims, the more profitable will be the undertakings and the more assured the results.

3. If thou do good to one, thou dost the good work of one; if thou do good to society, thou dost the good work of a whole society.

4. That which healeth a few for a day, is a poor remedy; but that which helpeth many to help themselves for a long time, is a great means.

5. Oh Charity which art skilled to teach, show My disciple the art of loving!

6. I have placed thee in My Church, that thou mayest do much good: see, My son, thou learn to do it well.

7. He who aimeth only at doing good to himself, will often reap no fruit.

8. If two undertake a good work and help each other, they will of a certainty gain some profit.

9. But if many serve Me with a pure intention, their undertakings will be as a rich and strong city.

10. Nothing more promoteth success than due obedience.

11. The more universal a good is, the more it possesseth of the divine and heavenly.

12. The more simple the means, the more efficient they are.

13. The less thou think of thyself, the more will others combine with thee.

14. The more ye love one another, the less need will ye have of rules.

15. Much will ye effect by your works, if My grace make them powerful.

16. Oh Charity, enlighten My friends, that they may know how to love and to win over the enemy!

17. Oh Eternal Father, as it is by Me, with Me, and in Me that Thou receivest all honour and glory, so likewise, My Father, let all My disciples truly glorify Thee by Me, with Me and in Me.

18. Were they but one heart and one soul, how truly worthy would be their praise!

19. What will all the forces of Hell avail against those who love one another with a true love?

20. What can separate My disciples from My love, if they are pure, humble of heart, and upright in intention?

21. Oh Charity, which hast caused Me to die upon the Cross for Mine enemies, kindle My friend with thy flames!

22. How thou wouldst love thine enemy, didst thou contemplate Me crucified on Calvary!

23. I know what love and sorrow are; I know pain and sweetness.

24. Now thou art on fire with zeal, and

seeing so much wickedness in the world, thou wouldst call down fire from Heaven.

25. Now thou wouldst that thy fingers should hold thunder-bolts, and I would see magnets in thy hands.

26. Alas! I have so sought thee and singled thee out by My love, and although thou hast received so many of My favours, yet thou knowest not of what spirit thou art.

27. Oh Charity, thou canst pray for thine enemy, convert My friend!

28. He who loveth, encourageth not sin, but converteth sinners by My grace.

29. He who loveth, sanctioneth not error, but teacheth truth to false teachers.

30. He who loveth, fomenteth not vices, but busieth himself in removing occasions and scandals.

31. He who loveth, abandoneth not him who slumbereth in indifference, but arouseth him and disposeth good friends for him.

32. He who loveth, maketh himself ready for all things, serving all men, yet without sharing in any evil.

33. He who loveth, spendeth himself in bestowing benefits, and measureth not his services by their glory.

34. Lastly, he who loveth, hopeth all from

My power and bounty, knowing that it is useless to build without My grace.

35. Oh Charity, which couldst give Me a Body, that I might love with a Heart of flesh, grant to My beloved the bowels of true piety and true love.

CHAPTER XXII.

OF TEN MAXIMS OF WHICH I MUST NEVER LOSE SIGHT.

1. Son, if thou canst not answer the current objections of the unbeliever, nor clearly state the fundamental truths of the Faith, what good canst thou do?

2. If thou know not the most simple and urgent of the social problems of the day, whereon dost thou waste thy time?

3. Without much enlightenment and without good foundations of doctrine, thou wilt proclaim the truth, but a lie will put thee to confusion.

4. Better is one will, properly taught and directed, than many ill-balanced and highly-educated minds.

5. Better is one principle soundly grasped,

than many vague and contradictory reflections.

6. Better is it to begin at a seasonable time, than to work very hurriedly.

7. Better is it to follow up what is profitable, than to exhaust oneself over the doubtful.

8. Better is it to think of the morrow, than vainly to remember the past.

9. Much wilt thou learn by reflection; much will be taught thee by good works.

10. Outward ills will do thee little harm, if thou take precautions, and if thou guard thyself betimes from inward defects.

CHAPTER XXIII.

HOW I CAN LABOUR WITHOUT INJURING ANYONE.

1. The more thou lovest self-denial, the less wilt thou persist in maintaining disputes.

2. How desirest thou to triumph over thy determined foes, if thou exert thyself to disunite those I have given thee as friends?

3. Blessed are the upright and simple of heart, for they shall meet with many friends for the good Cause.

4. He who hath confusion within, easily and in all things findeth contradiction without.

5. Three things do I abhor in My disciple: that he take no interest in My Cause, that he defend it for his own interests, and that he watch over it so ill as to destroy the interests which My Cause defendeth.

6. If thou desire to work usefully with Me, see that thou combat thyself.

7. And if thou desire to labour with success, strive to obey well rather than to command.

8. Where zeal showeth bitterness, it is difficult to avoid sin.

9. If thy neighbour err through ignorance, help him with thy knowledge ;

10. But if he sin with false science, hinder the evil of his influence.

11. The best antidote to error is the practice of great virtues ;

12. And the first means to gain sinners is the constant practice of small virtues.

13. If thou desire to defend the Faith with success, wait until thou canst obey in the spirit of charity.

14. Very good is thy teaching, if thy humility and self-denial recommend it.

15. Very stable are thy principles, if they conform to the teaching of My Vicar on earth.

16. Who hath set thee to define and to judge? Watch that thy vanity seduce thee not.

17. Examine thy conscience, and then shalt thou answer Me.

CHAPTER XXIV.

HOW MUCH GOOD I CAN DO TO THE AFFLICTED AND THE POOR.

1. Dispose thy heart to listen to My words in the deepest silence.

2. Fix thine attention so that thou mayest hear Me as a loving servant.

3. He is a just man, who worketh for his own everlasting salvation, but he is a great and just man, who worketh for the salvation of his country.

4. He loveth in truth, who with loving words showeth deeds of charity.

5. He suffereth well, who never com-

plaineth of injuries he receiveth from his neighbour.

6. He can speak of peace and of love, who warreth against himself in order to unite men more closely to God.

7. Tell Me the victories that thou hast gained over thyself, and I will tell thee the virtues thou possessest.

8. Instead of wrestling with fury and abuse, fight My battle with reasoning, and even better with good works.

9. Enthusiastic words I hold of small account; true fervour is humble and showeth itself by labour.

10. He who loveth much, suffereth little, for true love sweeteneth all.

11. And if passion is blind to see the faults of the beloved, true love seeth them with great clearness, so that it may be able to sympathize with misery.

12. Ah, did thy heart but love Him Who hath loved thee from all eternity! In labouring for Him thou wouldst find thy rest.

13. I have done for thee what thou canst never do for Me, but I have placed the needy before thine eyes, that thou mayest do for them all that thou canst with thy prayers and thy labour.

14. He is poor indeed, who, knowing many things, falleth into great errors.

15. He is poor indeed, who, surrounded by disciples, forgetteth My teaching.

16. He is poor and wretched, who, possessing great power, is a slave to himself.

17. He is poor without remedy, who, glorying in his wickedness, taketh the way to Hell.

18. Of what avail is it to be rich, to be learned, to be foreseeing, to be great, if men have not the riches of My grace?

19. It is of great merit to do good to great sinners, to those poorest of the poor.

CHAPTER XXV.

HOW I CAN OVERCOME THE CRAFT OF THE WICKED, IF I LOVE GOD.

1. Not only in what is entirely holy must thou serve Me, but also, as I have told thee at other times, in many things wherein thou canst do Me great service.

2. If a work be good and profitable, do

not allow error and impiety to claim it as their own, as if they had gained a victory.

3. If thou canst consecrate it wholly to My service, delay not to do so, although it may cost thee labour and sacrifice.

4. But if thou canst not gain so much, thou must let Mine influence penetrate as far as thy conscience permitteth.

5. If thou canst only prevent error claiming it, while the work is good, do this for the Cause of thy God.

6. Thou wilt learn how to labour much for My Cause, if thou examine in what way and with what craftiness impiety obtaineth its victories.

7. When the wicked man cannot openly contend with Me, he striveth to lessen Mine influence.

8. When he can gain authority with utility and honour, he striveth to ignore Me altogether.

9. He maketh weapons of all lawful human interests to attack in front or in flank the Christian virtues.

10. Little by little, he leadeth the indifferent into disorder and perverteth him with much guile.

11. Do thou always the opposite, and thou wilt do much in a short time.

12. Thou must so combat thine adversary, that thou canst, if needed, put him to confusion.

13. Thou must so contend with thine enemy, that thou canst gain him and make of him a friend.

14. Thou must so guard thyself from the wicked, that thou canst become a messenger of God to him, if thou see him afflicted.

15. Ah! if thou hadst ardent charity, how much wouldst thou be able to love!

16. Love truly divine is chaste, is prudent, is kind, is persevering, is diligent, is subtle. It penetrateth to the heart of the sinner, of the impious, of him who perverteth, of him who seduceth, of him who lordeth and tyrannizeth; it helpeth him to rise from his wretched state, and to make himself holy with My grace.

17. Wherever thou art and workest with earnestness for My Cause, there will I be with thee, if thou merit that I should bless thine efforts.

CHAPTER XXVI.

HOW I MUST DIRECT MY INTENTION FOR THE GLORY OF CHRIST,

1. My true disciple and apostle, My son, in all things striveth to exalt Me; and the more he exalteth and glorifieth Me, the more must he acknowledge that I am greater than all honour and praise.

2. Cease not, therefore, to serve Me and to watch over My Cause.

3. But to direct thine intention and to put fervour into thy spirit, it is good that thy speech and thy affections accustom themselves to say frequently :

4. ℣. *Laudetur Jesus Christus :*

℞. *Ex hoc, nunc et usque in sæcula.*

5. ℣. Praise Jesus Christ,
    Ye lives and forces, bodies and souls :

℞. From this moment, now
    And to all eternity.   Amen.

6. ℣. Praise Jesus Christ,
    Ye works and sciences, letters and arts :

℞. From this moment, now
    And to all eternity.   Amen.

7. ℣. Praise Jesus Christ,
    Ye wise and gifted, ye saints and
       angels:
  ℟. From this moment, now
    And to all eternity. Amen.

8. ℣. Praise Jesus Christ,
    Ye ideals and intentions:
  ℟. From this moment, now
    And to all eternity. Amen.

9. ℣. Praise Jesus Christ,
    Ye energies and hopes:
  ℟. From this moment, now
    And to all eternity. Amen.

10. ℣. Praise Jesus Christ,
    Ye heroic acts and virtues:
  ℟. From this moment, now
    And to all eternity. Amen.

11. ℣. Praise Jesus Christ,
    Ye sacrifices and martyrdoms:
  ℟. From this moment, now
    And to all eternity. Amen.

12. ℣. Praise Jesus Christ,
    Ye societies and individuals:
  ℟. From this moment, now
    And to all eternity. Amen.

13. ℣. Praise Jesus Christ,
    Ye magistrates and rulers:
  ℟. From this moment, now
    And to all eternity. Amen.

14. ℣. Praise Jesus Christ,
    Ye laws, customs and governments:
    ℟. From this moment, now
    And to all eternity.   Amen.

15. ℣. Praise Jesus Christ,
    Ye peoples and nations, earth and
    heaven:
    ℟. From this moment, now
    And to all eternity.   Amen.

16. ℣. *Laudetur Jesus Christus,*
    ℟. *Ex hoc, nunc et usque in sæcula.*   Amen.

OTHER TITLES AVAILABLE

NOTES

NOTES

NOTES

NOTES

NOTES

NOTES

NOTES

NOTES

NOTES

NOTES